# Diversification and Development:
# The Case of Coffee

# Paul Streeten
# Diane Elson

The Praeger Special Studies program—utilizing the most modern and efficient book production techniques and a selective worldwide distribution network—makes available to the academic, government, and business communities significant, timely research in U.S. and international economic, social, and political development.

# Diversification and Development:
# The Case of Coffee

PRAEGER SPECIAL STUDIES IN INTERNATIONAL ECONOMICS AND DEVELOPMENT

**raeger Publishers**  New York  Washington  London

PRAEGER PUBLISHERS
111 Fourth Avenue, New York, N.Y. 10003, U.S.A.
5, Cromwell Place, London S.W.7, England

Published in the United States of America in 1971
by Praeger Publishers, Inc.

Library of Congress Catalog Card Number: 76-163931

Printed in the United States of America

# ACKNOWLEDGMENTS

This book grew out of work Mr. Streeten did in Rome during the winter of 1967 for a joint study by the International Bank for Reconstruction and Development, the International Coffee Organization and the Food and Agriculture Organization of the United Nations, under the direction of Dr. Gerda Blau. He owes encouragement and many ideas to Dr. Blau's brilliant insight, though she obviously is not responsible for any errors or faults. Mrs. Muriel Payne patiently typed the manuscripts.

# CONTENTS

LIST OF TABLES AND FIGURES

FIGURE

# Diversification and Development: The Case of Coffee

# THE INTERNATIONAL DIMENSIONS
# OF THE COFFEE PROBLEM

There are very few tropical less-developed countries that do not grow coffee. Its significance, however, depends not so much on the value of its total production, which is small in relation to many agricultural products, as upon the high proportion of its production that is internationally traded.*

Moreover, the major exporters of coffee tend to be highly dependent on it for foreign exchange earnings (see Table 1). For most less-developed countries, foreign exchange earnings are of critical importance as a means of purchasing imports required for their economic development. Failure to achieve an adequate and stable growth of these earnings may prove to be a critical constraint on their ability to implement development plans. Thus, for at least ten countries in Latin America and Africa, coffee is of vital importance.

## A PROBLEM COMMODITY

Unfortunately, for these countries coffee is a "problem" commodity. To begin with, it suffers from considerable short-run price instability. Short-term fluctuations in primary commodity prices are complex in character and origin. Daily and weekly fluctuations are more likely to reflect random factors, while monthly and annual changes tend very largely to reflect intra- and inter-seasonal changes. For coffee there is a tendency for a year of very high production to be followed by one of very low produc-

*Generally between 60 per cent and 80 per cent in the postwar period.

TABLE 1

The Importance of Coffee Exports
to Some Major Exporters

|  | Average percentage of domestic merchandize export earnings supplied by coffee 1963-67* |
| --- | --- |
| Brazil | 47.5 |
| Colombia | 67.3 |
| El Salvador | 49.0 |
| Guatemala | 44.9 |
| Angola | 47.1 |
| Ethiopia | 58.6 |
| Ivory Coast | 38.9 |
| Kenya | 20.3 |
| Tanzania | 14.2 |
| Uganda | 45.1 |

*This was substantially the period covered by the first International Coffee Agreement.

Source: Commonwealth Secretariat, Plantation Crops, No. 12 (1969), p. 34.

tion (and vice versa). The annual fluctuations for coffee, although not as large as for many primary products, are nevertheless quite substantial. A United Nations study for the period 1950-61 shows that the average year-to-year fluctuations of unit export value of coffee were 9 per cent and of export proceeds 8 per cent.[1] Such variability in export proceeds may handicap growth by the disruption of investment and production plans. However, during the decade 1947-57, coffee-exporting countries had the consolation that their earnings were on average growing considerably faster than those of any other group of primary producing countries, except those exporting petroleum.[2]

Unfortunately this happy state of affairs did not last. Besides short-term fluctuations, coffee is also subject to a longer cyclical pattern, which derives its dynamic essentially from the interplay between prices and production. By contrast, the swings in world consumption have been relatively small, except for the disruptions of war time. In addition, consumption is not very responsive to price changes, especially to price falls. The Food and Agriculture Organization (F.A.O.) has estimated that for higher-income countries the price elasticity of demand for coffee lies between -0.2 and -0.3, and for lower-income countries between -0.4 and -0.6.[3] There is a certain amount of evidence that a large and prolonged price rise might have more effect on demand. As a result of the price boom of 1954, American consumers seem to have reduced the strength, although not the number, of their cups of coffee. Before the boom it is estimated that they brewed about 40 cups per pound; after the boom just over 60 cups per pound.[4] However, on the whole, coffee drinking is a matter of habit that takes time to change. Consumption seems to be more affected by changes in income and the standard of living than by changes in price.

The relationship between production and prices is much more complicated. A rise in the world price of coffee can be met in the short-run by more intensive harvesting of the coffee cherries, and by more intensive cultivation and greater use of fertilizer, insecticide, etc., and a consequent rise in yields. If this increase in supply is not sufficient to stabilize the price level, it generally results in the planting of new (and possibly improved) coffee trees. However, the new trees do not mature rapidly: New plantings begin to bear in 2 to 4 years if seedlings are used, and in 4 to 5 years if plantings are from seeds. Substantial crops cannot be expected until, say, 5 to 8 years after a new plantation is established, with yields rising to a maximum after 10 to 15 years. So for at least 4 to 5 years after new planting has begun, prices are likely to continue high, thus inducing continued new planting. Once a substantial number of young trees begin to bear fruit, supply for the market will greatly increase, and prices will begin to weaken. This discourages new planting and eventually brings it to an end.

However, the market does not reach a new equilibrium there, at the point where net investment has ceased. Production goes on rising for some years as trees of a later vintage bear fruit and this forces the price down further. Unfortunately, however, this fall in price has little immediate effect in choking off supply. Most costs are fixed to the producers--land rent, capital in the form of trees, the salary of the manager on plantations--and variable costs, particularly labor costs, are very low. Producers will continue cultivation as long as receipts cover their variable costs, and, given the cost structure of the coffee industry, this will occur even at very low ex-farm prices. This is particularly true of producers in Africa whose "out of pocket" production costs are very low, and who have little incentive to shift to alternative crops. Low prices have seldom induced growers to go to the expense of uprooting trees that are still yielding and to plant other crops, and since coffee trees have a productive life of 25 years or longer, adjustment will clearly not be rapid. Eventually of course receipts must cover full costs or the producer will leave the industry, but this is unlikely to happen before the country has suffered a very large fall in export receipts.

Thus there are two major factors making coffee a "problem" commodity. Because of the lag in the production process, supply response to a sustained price rise tends to overshoot the mark; and because of the cost structure, the subsequent fall in price can be sustained for quite a long time before it has a substantial effect upon supply.

## PRICES AND PRODUCTION

This interaction of prices and production can be seen at work in the post-World War II period. In the early postwar period, the exhaustion of Brazilian stocks, rising European demand and stagnation in production (coupled with a certain amount of market speculation) led to a sharp rise in prices in 1950 (see Table 2). However, prices in New York rose by more than 50 per cent in that one year.

The removal of United States price control in 1953, and frost in some Brazilian coffee-producing areas, was followed by a new wave of price advances, reaching a sharp peak in 1954, when prices had almost trebled from their 1948 level.  Under this stimulus a period of intense planting began, in particular in the Paraná district of Brazil, and in Africa where large areas of jungle were cleared for coffee.  There was less new planting in Latin America outside Brazil, in some cases because of the shortage of unused good-quality coffee land, but efforts were made to increase production through the rehabilitation of old plantations and better cultivation methods.

By 1956 this was beginning to have an impact on the market.  World production increased sharply, and, for the first time since the end of the war, the Brazilian government began to purchase coffee for stockpiling.  The crop in 1957 was affected by frost and fell back to the level of 1955, but after 1957 coffee production rose by leaps and bounds.  Unfortunately consumption was growing much more slowly. Stock buying became a regular feature of the coffee market, but even this did not prevent world prices from falling sharply after 1957.  This fall in prices reduced total earnings from coffee exports by about a fifth between 1956 and 1959, a considerable blow to the coffee-producing countries.[5]  However, there was no sign of any cutback in production:  1960 saw a record crop of over 78 million bags.  Although this was not maintained, production continued at high levels in the early 1960's.  It has been estimated that a price reduction of 45 per cent would have been necessary to absorb the annual surplus of some 600,000 metric tons produced in 1961-63, before making any provision for the reduction of accumulated stocks, which by that time were about equal to annual exportable production.[6]

## INTERNATIONAL COFFEE AGREEMENTS

The industry was clearly in difficulties, but producing countries were unwilling to let world prices go on falling until supply and demand were

TABLE 2

Prices, Production and Stocks of Coffee

| | Prices[a] (U.S. cents per lb.) | | | World Production[b] (1000 bags) | Stocks[c] (1000 bags) |
|---|---|---|---|---|---|
| | Santos 4 | Manizales | Native Uganda | | |
| 1948 | 27.1 | 32.5 | 17.8 | ... | ... |
| 1949 | 32.8 | 37.4 | 18.9 | ... | ... |
| 1950 | 50.5 | 53.2 | 40.1 | 37,897 | 10,027 |
| 1951 | 54.2 | 58.7 | 46.8 | 38,112 | 8,133 |
| 1952 | 54.0 | 57.0 | 44.0 | 39,862 | 6,541 |
| 1953 | 57.9 | 60.2 | 47.6 | 41,729 | 5,273 |
| 1954 | 78.7 | 80.0 | 57.9 | 42,414 | 5,611 |
| 1955 | 57.1 | 64.6 | 38.4 | 42,587 | 6,493 |
| 1956 | 58.1 | 74.0 | 33.6 | 51,881 | 11,196 |
| 1957 | 56.9 | 63.9 | 34.6 | 42,527 | 16,517 |
| 1958 | 48.4 | 52.3 | 37.6 | 55,788 | 14,956 |
| 1959 | 37.0 | 45.2 | 28.7 | 63,716 | 23,846 |
| 1960 | 36.6 | 44.9 | 20.2 | 78,356 | 36,870 |
| 1961 | 36.0 | 43.6 | 18.5 | 67,223 | 60,940 |

| 1962 | 34.0 | 40.8 | 20.6 | 73,795 | 66,534 |
| 1963 | 34.1 | 39.5 | 27.9 | 69,759 | 72,448 |
| 1964 | 46.7 | 48.8 | 35.6 | 66,781 | 70,655 |
| 1965 | 44.7 | 48.5 | 31.1 | 62,494 | 78,342 |
| 1966 | 40.8 | 47.4 | 33.6 | 81,057 | 69,543 |
| 1967 | 37.8 | 41.8 | 33.5 | 64,125 | 87,450 |
| 1968 | 37.4 | 42.6 | 34.0 | ... | ... |

aAnnual average spot prices for the three main types of coffee on the New York market.

bA bag weighs 60 kg. This is the usual standard unit in the coffee industry.

cStocks held at June 30, the beginning of the coffee year.

Sources: For Prices, 1948-60: FAO, The World Coffee Economy, C.B.S. 33, (1961); 1960-68: FAO, Monthly Bulletin of Agricultural Economics and Statistics (December 1968 and December 1969).
    For Production and Stocks: Keith Griffin, "Reform and Diversification in a Coffee Economy: The Case of Guatemala" in (ed. Paul Streeten) Unfashionable Economics (London: Weidenfeld and Nicolson, 1970), p. 78.

once again in balance because of the potentially
disastrous fall in foreign exchange earnings that
this would entail.  Several producer agreements
designed to limit exports on a yearly basis were set
up, beginning in 1957.  At first only Latin American
countries entered into these agreements, but they
were joined by French and Portuguese African dependen-
cies in 1959 and by U.K. - associated territories in
1960.  But these were merely agreements between
producing nations, and as such, subject to risk of
members suddenly leaving them.  But eventually in
1962 an International Coffee Agreement including
major importers as well as exporters was concluded.
It obtained the acceptance of countries accounting
for 97.4 per cent of world coffee exports and 96
per cent of imports.

The chief object of this Agreement was price
support rather than price stabilization:  It was
designed to increase receipts from coffee exports
by preventing world prices from falling below the
1962 level.  This was to be achieved primarily by
imposing quotas on exports to traditional markets
in North America and Western Europe, the so-called
Annex A countries.  Exports to new markets, the
so-called Annex B countries, chiefly in Eastern
Europe and the underdeveloped countries, were free
from quotas.  A basic quota was allocated to each
exporting country, and annual quotas expressed as a
uniform percentage of the basic quota were to be
assigned to each country on the basis of estimates
of world production and imports.  Each producing
country was free to decide for itself how it would
comply with the quota agreement.  The importing
countries were expected to play a key role in enforc-
ing the Agreement by requiring certificates of origin
for all imported coffee and by checking to see that
each bag of coffee had the requisite number of export
stamps.  It has not been possible to close all the
loopholes; in particular it has not been possible
to prevent the appearance since late 1965 of substantial quantities of "tourist" coffee, i.e., coffee
that changes its destination in mid-ocean, or is
re-exported from one of the Annex B countries.

The Agreement was certainly successful in preventing prices from falling below their 1962 level,
but it was unable to maintain prices at the higher
levels experienced in 1964 and 1965. Thus in 1966,
when prices of Latin American coffees fell quite
sharply, the International Coffee Council introduced
some elements of selective adjustment in an attempt
to stabilize prices. Selectivity did not apply to
annual quotas that were still determined at a uniform
rate, but only to special export authorizations and
waivers permitting exports additional to annual
quotas. All coffees were arranged in four groups,
each with its own indicator price range. If the
average of the daily prices of any group over a
period of 15 consecutive market days fell below the
"floor" price or rose above the "ceiling" price for
that group, the special export authorizations and
waivers for all members of that group were to be
adjusted--upward in the case for price rise, downward
in the case of price fall. The adjustment was to
be equal to 2.5 per cent of their total authorized
exports on October 1, 1966, but as this did not
prove a sufficient margin of change, various quantities
of coffee were subsequently transferred from annual
quotas, which cannot be altered under the selective
system, to the special export authorizations which
can be adjusted.

In 1968 the Agreement was renewed, along the
same lines as before, although the basic quotas were
revised. The selective adjustments to price changes
were also to be continued on much the same basis
as before, only limiting the amount by which annual
quotas may be reduced to 5 per cent.

This kind of agreement operates essentially by
preventing prices from clearing the market, and by
freezing the current price and production structure
(although changes can be made when quotas are revised).
It is frequently argued that the only way to a
fundamental solution to the coffee problem, by which
is meant bringing world supply and demand more nearly
into equilibrium and yet ensuring an adequate supply
of foreign exchange to coffee producing countries,

is production control and diversification.  Both
International Coffee Agreements have paid lip service
to the need for production control, but attempts
to lay down precise targets for individual countries,
let alone secure compliance with them, have come to
nothing.  A Diversification Fund to which all exporting members must subscribe was perhaps the major
innovation of the 1965 Agreement.  But the implications
for national policies of production control and
diversification require further analysis.


## NOTES

1.   United Nations, World Economic Survey, 1963
(New York: 1964), quoted in Keith Griffin, Under-
development in Spanish America (London: Allen and
Unwin, 1969), p. 104.

2.   Food and Agriculture Organization (FAO)
The World Coffee Economy, Commodity Bulletin Series
(C.B.S.) 33 (1961), p. 1.

3.   Ibid., p. 31.

4.   J. W. F. Rowe, The World's Coffee (London:
H.M.S.O., 1963), p. 25.

5.   FAO, op. cit., p. 7.

6.   FAO, Agricultural Commodities--Projections
for 1975 and 1985, Vol. 1 (Oct. 1966), pp. 239-241
quoted by Keith Griffin "Reform and Diversification
in a Coffee Economy:  The Case of Guatemala" in (ed.
Paul Streeten) Unfashionable Economics (London:
Weidenfeld and Nicolson, 1970), p. 78.

# 2

## NATIONAL COFFEE POLICY:
## PRODUCTION CONTROL AND DIVERSIFICATION

At the most general level, successful development
and the "solution" of the coffee problem are interdependent:  Only accelerated development generates
the employment opportunities (i.e., the markets and
the necessary complementary factors of production)
that will induce some coffee producers to prefer
higher-yielding and more-dynamic occupations.  It
can also be argued, although less cogently, that
contraction* of coffee production is a condition of
development because it releases resources to other
more productive uses and thus reduces a country's
dependence on a limited and precarious source of
export earnings, subject to international restrictions.

### CONTRACTION OF PRODUCTION AS A CONDITION
### OF DEVELOPMENT

There are two weaknesses in this second half of
the interdependence between development and coffee
contraction.  First, although it may be in the interest of world coffee producers as a group to limit
production, the same is not true of any one country's
producers.  There is always the possibility of inducing consumers to switch from one source to another,
enabling one country or group of countries to benefit
at the expense of another.  In the fifties for instance, African countries expanded production more
rapidly than Latin American countries and succeeded
in considerably increasing their share of the export
market (see Table 3).  Even when an International

*In the following, "contract" or "limit" coffee
production should be interpreted as reducing production below what it otherwise would have been, not
necessarily below past production.

TABLE 3

Percentage Distribution of Coffee Production and Exports

| | 1946-60 | | 1951-55 | | 1956-60 | |
|---|---|---|---|---|---|---|
| | Production | Exports | Production | Exports | Production | Exports |
| North and Central America | 16.2 | 12.5 | 16.3 | 15.0 | 14.4 | 15.8 |
| South America | 68.9 | 73.2 | 64.4 | 65.0 | 64.5 | 57.7 |
| Africa | 11.7 | 13.4 | 15.2 | 17.8 | 17.1 | 23.7 |

Source: FAO, The World Coffee Economy, C.B.S. 33 (1961), pp. 48 and 58.

24

Agreement is operating it remains true that a given
country's development prospects may be improved by
higher coffee production.  Within the Agreement,
expansion of coffee capacity may add to a country's
bargaining power for an increase in its quota at
future negotiations.  The figures in Table 4 suggest
this may have been the case.

   Outside the Agreement it also makes sense:  A
country may hope to raise the value of its sales by
slightly undercutting the agreed price.  Moreover,
a country may wish to take account of the possibility
of a future abandonment of the Agreement.  For such
reasons it would not be legitimate to assume, without
further argument, that limitation is necessarily
always in the interest of the producers of any particular country.

   The second weakness is that a reduction in coffee
production is not a condition of development in the
sense that it would normally release many scarce
productive factors.  For a proper understanding of
the problem, Professor Hla Myint's reminder and re-
interpretation of Adam Smith's "vent for surplus"
theory provides a number of clues.[1]  In contrast to
the theory of comparative costs, it assumes not given
and fully employed resources that can be devoted to
either domestic use or trade, but instead the existence of surplus productive capacity of a specific
kind.  The function of international trade is to
provide not incentives for a more efficient reallocation of resources, but effective demand for the output of the surplus resources, which would not have
been used at all or used much less productively (or
at excessive costs) in the absence of trade.  In
such a situation, exports do not reduce domestic
production.

   The notion of the surplus implies either or
both of two conditions:  price inelasticity of domestic demand for the exportable product and specificity
of resources producing it.  In contrast, much of
the reasoning about alternatives for coffee is based,
implicitly or explicitly, on the theory of comparative
costs, which assumes high domestic price elasticities
of demand and/or flexibility and mobility of resources.

TABLE 4

Percentage Distribution of Coffee Production and Export Quotas

| | Production | | Quotas | |
| | Average 1962-63 | Average 1966-67 | First Agreement | Second Agreement |
|---|---|---|---|---|
| Brazil | 47.0 | 40.0 | 39.1 | 38.0 |
| Other Latin American[a] | 22.1 | 22.9 | 24.5 | 24.7 |
| Africa[b] | 18.3 | 22.2 | 22.9 | 25.8 |

[a]Columbia, El Salvador, Guatemala, Mexico, Costa Rica.

[b]Ivory Coast, Cameroun, Malagasy, Uganda, Kenya, Tanzania, Angola, Ethiopia, Congo (Kinshasa).

Sources: Distribution of production: Commonwealth Secretariat, Plantation Crops, No. 12 (1969), Table 3, p. 23.

Distribution of quotas: Commonwealth Secretariat, Plantation Crops, No. 12 (1969), p. 220.

Coffee production methods are still primitive
in many areas. The use of chemical organic fertilizers, of mulching and of irrigation is still limited
on estates and not very common on smallholdings.[2]
The two main inputs into coffee production are unskilled labor and land, and either or both of these
are abundant in many of the major coffee producing
countries, particularly where the peasant sector is
important. (Contrary to the common belief that coffee
is almost everywhere an estate crop, it is in fact
mainly grown by smallholders--although plantations
are responsible for the greater part of output of
some important exporting countries such as Angola,
Brazil and Guatemala.)[3] The seasonal work pattern
of coffee production can be dovetailed with that of
subsistence agriculture, or·additional migratory
labor can be obtained for seasonal peaks. In such
circumstances to limit coffee production may result
in even greater unemployment and land lying fallow.[4]

The initial situation of surplus arises because
at low levels of development there is an imbalance
between resources and demand. The equilibrating
mechanisms presupposed by the theory of comparative
costs in its Heckscher-Ohlin version* are absent
in an economy in which the subsistence sector is
large. This theory assumes flexible prices to which
producers and consumers respond, mobile resources,
seeking the highest reward, and a wide spectrum of
substitutable techniques and commodities, combining
factors in different proportions according to price
and income signals and incentives. These conditions,
which are supposed to be the cause of international
trade and development, are in fact their result.
Hence the coexistence of surplus productive capacity
with low income levels in underdeveloped countries.

---

*This version assumes that different countries
have different relative factor endowments, but the
same production functions, whereas the Ricardo version
assumes that they have similar endowments but different production functions.

The argument calls for a number of qualifications.
First, the "vent for surplus" interpretation fits
best the peasant smallholder sector in some countries.
In the large plantations and estates, indigenous land
and labor are combined with additional capital and
management, sometimes foreign. Even although capital
and management are attracted by the existence of
surplus labor and land, they are, of course, themselves
not in surplus and have positive and sometimes high
opportunity costs, though not normally in terms of
domestic alternatives. Foreign capital is mobile
internationally and contraction of coffee plantations
does not necessarily imply reallocation to domestic
food production. It has been easy to attract foreign
capital into plantations and notoriously difficult
to attract it for domestic food production. Even
indigenous capital, if it can find a way, may emigrate
in preference to engaging in domestic alternatives.
We shall discuss below a proposal to overcome some
obstacles.

Second, even in the peasant export sector, the
potential surplus becomes actual only after adequate
provision of transport, communications and marketing
facilities. Some scarce inputs with alternative uses
may be employed in this sector also, such as fertilizers. If the intensity of coffee cultivation is
stepped up beyond a certain point, it may compete
with food production in seasonal peaks. But it would
not be correct to consider the sacrifice of peasant
leisure as an opportunity cost, if such leisure is
not "voluntary."

## IMPLICATIONS OF SURPLUS CAPACITY

The existence of such actual or potential surplus
capacity in land and labor can be regarded as an advantage or as a disadvantage for the trading country.
It is an advantage because it provides, at low or
zero domestic opportunity costs, a source of domestic
incomes, savings, foreign exchange, fiscal revenue
and perhaps various linkages. The economic history
of Brazil illustrates how this sector can make a
vital contribution to industrialization and

development.  If the country is fortunate and there
is a large and expanding foreign demand for its
surplus exports the surplus sector can become a
leading sector.  In conjunction with appropriate
human responses, social institutions adapted to
these responses and public policies, the surplus
sector can provide an important source of development
and hence of introducing precisely those flexibili-
ties and mobilities whose absence caused the orig-
inal imbalance.  Such was the case with textile
exports in industrializing England and coffee exports
in Brazil.  Today, some oil-producing and mining
countries enjoy similar forms of export-led development.

On the other hand, it is a disadvantage, because
if foreign demand is limited or reduced, a switch
to alternatives is difficult or impossible and this
makes the country particularly vulnerable.  Such
a situation illustrates the potential benefits and
drawbacks of one type of unbalanced development.
It is also difficult to establish international
criteria for the allocation of production in these
circumstances.

It follows that coffee-producing units with
positive and substantial opportunity costs of at
least some of the factors employed by them, such
as plantations, must be treated differently from
subsistence farmers.  At first it would seem that,
given the need for contraction, resources that are
mobile should be moved.  But the situation is complicated by the fact that plantations might produce
at lower costs or, even when they are high-cost
producers, may be producing at falling costs because
they can afford to be more responsive to technical
improvements.  They also may carry the costs of
innovation which, if successful, can be imitated
by the smallholders and they should be credited with
these external economies.  In addition, if the
plantations are foreign-owned, their resources may
leave the country altogether rather than move into
domestic food production, so that the national
opportunity cost would be zero.

One may be faced with the dilemma that the low
or zero opportunity cost producers have neither
means nor incentives to lower costs and may be high
absolute cost producers, while the high opportunity
cost producers are those who are bringing their own
or other growers' costs down and tend to be or to
become low absolute cost producers.  If it is desired
to have, in the long run, an efficient coffee growing
industry, the decision as to who should contract will
depend (1) upon the time preference between low-cost
production now and over a series of future dates and
(2) upon the external economies of innovation and its
spread effects.

Since international cost comparisons, based
on comparative costs, become impossible, it might be
thought that in a "vent for surplus" situation
absolute cost comparison should be made.  But although
these might be possible, they are irrelevant for the
purpose of determining country quotas.  There is no
reason to say that a given world quota should be
filled by those with the lowest production costs.
If different producers operate with different costs,
the low-cost producers will get more out of the price
increases resulting from the restrictions than the
high-cost producers.  But on grounds of fair shares,
this might be used as an argument for giving the
high-cost producers a larger share.  It is, of course,
true that the low-cost producers have less to fear
from a breakdown of the Agreement and that therefore
their bargaining power is stronger.  But high-cost
producers can counter this by accumulating stocks.
It therefore appears to be impossible to derive
international criteria for allocation of production
either from opportunity costs or from absolute costs
as far as the smallholding coffee sector is concerned.

The existence of surplus capacity is itself a
function of the level of development.  The abundance
and low opportunity costs of many factors engaged
in coffee production are the result of general underdevelopment.  Successful development, which initially
need not compete with coffee production, will create
the conditions in which it will be easier to contract

the production of coffee.  In other words, opportunity
costs and mobility of resources are a function of
the development efforts of the country and the
opportunities provided by the world economy.


## DIVERSIFICATION

Therefore, although the solution of the coffee
problem and development are interdependent, it is
development that is the dominant partner in this
mutual relationship.  In other words, while it is
broadly true both that countries are poor because
they are not diversified (and therefore particularly
vulnerable to changes in technology and demand) and
that they are not diversified because they are poor,
the more fundamental of the two relations is the
second.  Diversification* is not so much the <u>condition</u>
of successful development, it is its <u>result</u>.  Adapta-
bility and alertness in deriving benefits from trade
are the result of progress.

It follows that a discussion of diversification
in the narrow sense, i.e., of the alternatives to
which the actual land and people employed in growing
coffee, or in agriculture generally, should be
diverted, is of only limited interest.  It would
give too narrow a picture and would obscure the
primacy of general development which, moreover, can
in many places proceed for some time without drawing
on factors engaged in coffee growing.  Contraction
of coffee production is often not a condition of
diversification at the farm level.  Where there is
underutilized labor and uncultivated land, such as
on the latifundia in Latin America, and in Tanzania,
a coffee farm can easily produce more of other types
of crops without reducing its output of coffee,

---

*The meaning of this much used and abused term
is not always clear.  In the present context all
that is meant is ability to respond quickly and at
low costs to changes in world demand and to seize
efficiently new production and export opportunities.

provided of course there are the right incentives,
infrastructure, etc.  On the other hand, it is quite
conceivable that from an economic point of view
the expansion of agricultural activities other than
coffee growing should take place outside the coffee
regions.  But just as possibilities for action and
investment within the entire agricultural sector
must be examined, so, too, activities outside agriculture should be considered.  Thus ultimately policies
for diversification are necessarily concerned with
the general strategy for economic development.

It follows that, apart from considerations of
income distribution, the most fundamental question
to ask is not what should coffee producers do, or
even to what use should land in agriculture be put,
but what are the development priorities for a country
wishing to accelerate its growth if an increase in
coffee production is ruled out.

## NOTES

1.  Hla Myint, "The 'Classical Theory' of
International Trade and the Underdeveloped Countries,"
Economic Journal, Vol. LXVIII, No. 68 (June 1958),
pp. 317-37.

2.  FAO, World Coffee Survey (Rome: FAO Agricultural Studies No. 76, 1968), p. 440.

3.  Ibid., p. 438.

4.  This appears to have happened in Brazil as
a result of the coffee eradication program.  See
Keith Griffin and E.F. Szczepanik "Diversification
Programs in Coffee Producing Countries" (mimeo.,
1968), p. 8--in a joint study by the International
Bank for Reconstruction and Development, the Inter-
national Coffee Organization, and the Food and
Agricultural Organization.

CHAPTER

# 3

## THE UTILIZATION OF LABOR

Most of the major coffee-growing countries have what is commonly described as a serious and growing problem of surplus labor, unemployment, disguised unemployment and underemployment. Whatever the precise interpretation of these somewhat vague and ill-defined terms, there can be no doubt that development policies must give a high priority to a fuller mobilization and utilization of what is sometimes thought to be their most abundant factor of production--unskilled labor.

UNEMPLOYMENT, UNDEREMPLOYMENT AND
DISGUISED UNEMPLOYMENT

To begin with, it is worth considering briefly the notions of unemployment, underemployment and disguised unemployment. In her well-known essay on disguised unemployment, Joan Robinson coined this term for a situation widely observed in the Great Depression, in which men, thrown out of regular employment, crowd into occupations like carrying bags, rendering small services or selling matches in the street.[1] The reasoning can best be brought out by a simple two-sector model: In one sector money wages are rigid downward, in the other, where self-employment prevails, incomes are flexible. In competitive full employment equilibrium, the marginal productivity of labor is the same in both sectors. If then a fall in aggregate demand below the full employment level occurs, men will be thrown out of work in the rigid wage sector but, rather than become unemployed, will move into the flexible income sector. Money income per man in this sector will fall as more men are accommodated to spread a smaller work load. Productivity differentials (measured in terms of man-years, man-weeks or man-days, but not in terms of man-hours, for productivity of hours

<u>not</u> worked is not meaningful) will increase, but no
visible unemployment will appear. The difference
between a situation of general low labor productivity
(say due to absence of skills or low investment per
worker) and a situation of disguised unemployment
in this sense is that a rise in the level of effective
demand will shift workers back into the high-productivity, rigid-wage sector and remove the disguised
unemployment. The workers are adapted to the requirements in this sector and, if the time spent in the
flexible-income sector has not been too long, so
that they have not forgotten their skills, have
remained well fed and healthy and have not been de-
moralized, a rise in effective demand is sufficient
to restore full employment equilibrium.

Although the two sectors have certain features
in common with the "modern" and the "traditional"
sectors in less-developed countries, it is obvious
that the situation in the rural sector of developing
countries is quite different from that described by
Joan Robinson. It is true that the rural subsistence
sector, in which smallholdings are cultivated by
families, resembles the flexible income sector in
that it is capable of spreading a constant or slowly
growing work load and product over a rapidly growing
number of people. But it is not true that an increase
of effective demand would, by itself, absorb the excess population in industry. Neither is the provision
of equipment all that is needed to absorb labor and
raise production. In fact, a number of other measures
are necessary for a full mobilization and utilization
of manpower: better feeding, improvements in health,
training and education, transport and housing, and
fundamental attacks on prevailing attitudes to life
and work (e.g., women's participation, a contempt
for certain kinds of work, the desire to minimize
work, lack of discipline) and on institutions (the
introduction of a standard working week and working
day, the creation of a labor market, the provision
of information, the ability to move from one place
to another or to change one's occupation, etc.)

As a first step in analysis, it is helpful to
break down the multiplicity of dimensions of income
(or product) per head of the population into four

categories.  These should aid the collection of data, the organization of thought and the formulation of policies.[2]

$$\frac{Income}{Population} = \frac{Production}{Hours\ Worked} \times \frac{Hours\ Worked}{Labor\ Force} \times$$

$$\frac{Labor\ Force}{People\ of\ Working\ Age} \times$$

$$\frac{People\ of\ Working\ Age}{Population}$$

The identity brings out four distinct aspects of the level of living (= income per head) on which more information would be useful for framing policies for the multidimensional aspects of labor utilization. It is important to note that the ratios are not independent of one another.

[1]        $\frac{Production}{Hours\ Worked}$  or hourly productivity

depends, in any given activity in any given sector, on a large number of factors (including other terms in the identity), such as: hours worked and participation rate (see below [2] and [3]); also on equipment, fuel, raw materials and other complementary productive factors; education and training; health affecting work such as intestinal parasites, amoebas, onchocerciasis or schistosomiasis; intensity of application, itself a function of morale; industrial relations; motivation; incentives, etc.; organization of work, management, etc.

This category covers numerous aspects, some of the most important of which are difficult to measure. For the country as a whole, it is an average of all sectors, each weighted by its share in the total number of hours worked.  If we denote the sectors as 1, 2, 3, etc., and their shares in total working hours as $h_1$, $h_2$, etc., we may write:

$$\frac{Output}{Hours\ Worked} = h_1 \frac{Y_1}{H_1} + h_2 \frac{Y_2}{H_2} + \dots$$

Hourly productivity can be raised if all other things

remain constant, either by transferring workers from
low-productivity to high-productivity sectors, or by
raising productivity within sectors.

[2]        $\dfrac{\text{Hours Worked}}{\text{Labor Force}}$ or working-time rate

depends on organizational and institutional factors:
whether there is a standard working day and working
week; whether overtime is worked; whether multiple
shifts exists; whether time is wasted in idleness,
waiting for materials and components, or spent on
holidays, weddings, funerals and at feasts.  It also
depends on natural factors such as the weather and
the requirements of harvest seasons.  The ratio will
depend both upon the level of demand and on the availability of essential supplies.  A shift of rural labor
to urban industry raises output not only by changing
the weights attached to low- and high-productivity
sectors, but also by raising hours worked per labor
force.  Unemployment of people both willing and able
to work will show up as a low ratio of hours worked
to size of the labor force.  But the distinction
between ability to work and willingness to work outside the home may not always be easy to draw or even
logically legitimate.  Are women, in countries with
Moslem influence, unwilling to work or incapable of
working?[3]  Much time is spent in an underdeveloped
country moving from one place to another:  Peasants
walk from one piece of their land to another; women
walk back and forth to draw water; migrant workers
walk from one region to another to collect the harvest, etc.  Insofar as these movements are necessary
to carry out specific tasks, given the prevailing
institutions, transport facilities and cooperating
factors, it is a factor accounting for low hourly
productivity.  But if the movements are in search
of work, they come under low working time.

[3]        $\dfrac{\text{Labor Force}}{\text{People of Working Age}}$ or participation rate

depends on attitudes to work and to gainful activities
(their dignity or ignominy), housing and transport
facilities, legislation about minimum working age,
compulsory full-time education, etc.  Removal of the
objections to certain kinds of work, increased

incentives to earn money, emancipation of women, improved mobility, etc., will raise participation rates.

Education is by no means necessarily an investment with positive returns. It can result in reduced labor force participation. The educated unemployed, a widespread phenomenon in South Asia, figure prominently in unemployment statistics. While their geographical mobility between urban areas is high, their occupational mobility is small. They are not prepared to accept manual work. From a 1953 sample survey of unemployment in Calcutta it appears that only 10 percent of the unemployed were illiterate and 27 percent had enjoyed higher education. Only 43 percent of the total sample were seeking work involving manual labor.

The attitude to work appropriate for one who has enjoyed education is rooted in traditional attitudes and reinforced by the colonial heritage and possibly even by technical assistance. It is by no means just a matter of the wrong curriculum, for there is large and growing unemployment of engineers in India. It is estimated that there are now about 50,000 fully qualified engineers unemployed in 1970. The shortage exists in the same occupation for less qualified people, e.g., for semiskilled technicians.

Both in Asia and in Africa, education reflects and instills an antirural bias; indeed the pressures for education arise from a desire on the part of parents to free their children from the miseries and hardships of rural life.

Attitudes toward work among the educated--often ill-educated--are deeply rooted in the social structure and cannot easily be eliminated by restoring "equilibrium" between supply and demand, by changing curricula or by exhortation.

There are parallels between the participation rate of the unemployed and the participation rate of women. Nonparticipation of women is linked with status and prestige, particularly in the higher strata of society.

[4]    $\dfrac{\text{People of Working Age}}{\text{Population}}$ is a demographic ratio
and will depend on the age structure of the popula-
tion, which can be predicted with a fair degree of
accuracy. All those of working age in fourteen
years' time are already alive and only mortality and
migration rates have to be allowed for.

Since each of our four categories, viz., [1]
hourly productivity, [2] working time rate, [3] participation rate and [4] demographic ratio, is an
average of sectoral ratios, each sector appropriately
weighted, the identity can be rewritten as:

$$\frac{Y}{P} = \left[ h_1 \frac{Y_1}{H_1} + h_2 \frac{Y_2}{H_2} + \dots \right] \cdot \left[ l_1 \frac{H_1}{L_1} + l_2 \frac{H_2}{L_2} + \dots \right] \cdot$$

$$\left[ p_1 \frac{L_1}{W_1} + p_2 \frac{L_2}{W_2} + \dots \right] \cdot \left[ s_1 \frac{W_1}{P_1} + s_2 \frac{W_2}{P_2} + \dots \right]$$

where    Y is total income (output)
         H is total hours worked
         L is labor force
         W is working age group
         P is population
         h is share in total hours worked
         l is share in labor force
         p is share in age group
         s is share in population

and the suffixes indicate the different sectors.

The conventional presentation in terms of employment, unemployment and underployment suffers
from the fact that intensity of work, skill, organization, education, health, labor markets, transport,
information, etc., are assumed given. Thus the only
variables are demand and equipment. Furthermore,
the assumption is usually made that unemployment
and underemployment are "involuntary".[4] This implies
that willingness and ability to work are present.
It also presupposes labor exchanges or some other
objective test of voluntariness. Without such test,
it is impossible to tell. Some men work with
dysentery, others don't. Some may not seek work

because they know or believe that none is available.
In the absence of an organized market for labor, the
distinction between voluntary and involuntary unemployment breaks down.  Unemployment and underemployment must also be defined with reference to some
standard of working hours per day and working days
per week.  But such standards do not exist in large
parts of traditional societies and are therefore
introduced, usually implicitly, from outside.  The
whole set of questions relating to participation
and organized work is thereby begged and a number
of important relationships are concealed.  Once the
relevant distinctions are drawn, policies can then
be classified according to whether they use compul-
sive, permissive or persuasive measures.[5]  Table 5
provides illustrations.

The main lesson of this brief discussion is
that the utilization of labor in coffee-growing
developing countries has many dimensions and it is
not warranted to assume that attitudes, aptitudes
and institutions are adapted to full-labor utilization
or that consumption at low levels of living has no
effect on productivity.  Measures that raise labor
productivity may reduce hours worked or participation
rates[6] and measures that raise participation rates
may lead to work-spreading and less-intensive, or
to otherwise less-productive, work.  Only a simulta-
neous attack on several of the relevant variables
can bring about fuller utilization of labor.

The analysis also bears on the argument that
there is a surplus of unskilled labor to draw on
for any alternative activities to coffee production
and that labor opportunity costs are therefore low
or zero.  If these alternatives require attitudes,
motivations, responses, work habits or institutions
different from those to be found in coffee growing,
the fact that coffee growers have spare time left
over is irrelevant to the availability of this labor
time for these alternatives.  It would be dangerous
to argue from the premise that coffee growing does
not take up all the potential working hours of the
farmers to the conclusion that alternative work opportunities, either elsewhere or in the place of

TABLE 5

Classification of Measures to Induce
Participation in Organized Work

| | Compulsive | Permissive | Persuasive (incentives) |
|---|---|---|---|
| Output/Hour | Make pay depend on minimum output | Forbid trade union restrictions | Piece rates |
| Hours/Labor Force | Fix 8-hour day | Improve diet | Overtime rates |
| Labor Force/People of Working Age | Lock up workless, conscript, poll tax | Raise demand, provide equipment | Raise wages, supply incentive goods |
| People of Working Age/ Population | Draconian measures against large families, forced late marriage | Birth control advice and contraceptives supplied | Birth control campaigns, a transistor for a vasectomy, child tax |

residence, would automatically be taken up and result
in larger production.  Proposals for alternatives
must be accompanied by detailed specification as to
what measures of reform of human attitudes to work
and life and to social and commercial institutions,
such as land reform, or reform of the civil service,
or the creation of a labor market, or of credit
channels, or of marketing outlets, have to accompany
this shift in resources.

## UNDERUTILIZATION OF LABOR

The main causes of the gross underutilization
of labor are to be found in rural underemployment,
combined with an industrial sector that, though
often growing very rapidly in terms of production,
is too small and often uses techniques inappropriate
to absorb even a fraction of the rapidly growing
potential labor force.  Underutilization reflects
the attitudes and institutions of a backward society
and can therefore not be treated as a source for
its transformation through diversification.

At the same time, looking at the problem simply
from the point of view of rural surplus population,
it makes sense to ask the question:  How many people
can be removed from agriculture without reducing output?  For as Table 6 shows, in most of the major
coffee-exporting countries, well over half of the
economically active population is engaged in agriculture.  This is particularly pronounced in Africa:
In Tanzania 95 per cent of the economically active
population is engaged in agriculture.  This question
has been tackled by Rosenstein-Rodan, in a subtle
analysis, which distinguishes between two basic
concepts--the static and the dynamic--according to
whether methods of cultivation are assumed not to
change or whether they are assumed to change, when
the surplus population is removed, while output
remains constant.[7]

Rosenstein-Rodan claims that the static concept
is clear, whereas the dynamic concept requires a
detailed specification of what changes in methods

TABLE 6

Percentage of Economically Active
Population in Agriculture

| | |
|---|---|
| Brazil | 48 |
| Colombia | 47 |
| El Salvador | 59 |
| Guatemala | 64 |
| Angola | 82 |
| Ethiopia | 88 |
| Ivory Coast | 86 |
| Kenya | 88 |
| Tanzania | 95 |
| Uganda | 89 |

Source:   FAO, Production Yearbook (1969).

of cultivation are envisaged.  These changes might
vary from minor changes "obtained merely through a
rearrangement of work with but small additions of
circulating capital" to thoroughgoing and even
revolutionary changes, "including additional use
of both fixed and variable capital."[8]  The dynamic
concept, carried to the extreme, becomes irrelevant
for policy, because it raises questions such as what
would surplus population be if the agricultural
sector of an underdeveloped country were cultivated
under Dutch agricultural conditions.

In the context of the static concept, a distinction must be made between (1) removable disguised
underemployment; (2) disguised fractional underemployment, i.e., labor hours not used through the
year that do not add up to an entire labor unit
(these cannot be removed without a decline in output
but they can be provided with part-time work in
rural industries, rural public works, etc.); (3)
seasonal underemployment due to climatic factors.
In general, Rosenstein-Rodan concludes that where
there is dependence on one type of crop, the size
of the removable surplus is much greater.  Where
there are two or three crops a year most of the

population active in agriculture is employed for
more than 50 days a year, and it is probable that
few workers can be removed entirely from agriculture
if the same output is to be maintained without a
change in methods of production.* This may even be
the case in the most densely populated areas. The
approach to labor utilization must then run not in
terms of <u>alternatives</u> to agriculture, but <u>additional</u>
activities that would reduce rural underutilization
of labor.

## INDUSTRIALIZATION AS A SOLUTION

Much hope has been placed in the industrial
sector as a source of jobs for the growing labor
force. But the industrial sector, although often
growing very rapidly in terms of production, is
generally too small and often uses techniques and
wage rates inappropriate to absorb even a fraction
of the rapidly growing potential labor force. The
small base of the industrial sector is an important
reason for its limited capacity to create employment
opportunities and absorb the growing rural surplus
population. As Table 7 shows, only Brazil among the
major coffee exporters has a manufacturing output
at all comparable to agriculture output.

If 20 per cent of the labor force were employed
in manufacturing and 80 per cent outside it and population growth (assumed for simplicity to be identical
with the growth of the labor force) was 3 per cent,
employment opportunities in industry would have to
grow at 15 per cent in order to absorb only the
additions to the labor force, without reducing already
existing unemployment and underemployment. If only
10 per cent of the labor force was in manufacturing
industry, employment growth would have to be 30 per
cent.

---

*Although Rosenstein-Rodan does suggest that
if peak loads can be reorganized, the size of the
surplus population can be considerably increased--
doubled in Southern Italy.

TABLE 7

Percentage Distribution of Gross Domestic
Product in Some Coffee-Producing
Countries, 1965

| | Percentage of G.D.P.[a] contributed by | | | |
|---|---|---|---|---|
| | Agriculture[b] | Manufacturing[c] | Services[d] | Others[e] |
| Brazil | 28 | 23 | 48 | 2 |
| Colombia | 32 | 18 | 43 | 7 |
| El Salvador | 29 | 17 | 45 | 9 |
| Guatemala | 28 | 15 | 55 | 2 |
| Ethiopia[f] | 65 | 7 | 27 | 2 |
| Kenya[f] | 41 | 10 | 46 | 2 |
| Tanzania | 57 | 4 | 34 | 5 |
| Uganda | 59 | 8 | 30 | 4 |

[a]Based on data in prices of 1960
[b]Including forestry and fishing
[c]Including water and power
[d]Trade, finance, insurance, public administration and defense
[e]Residual including mining, construction, transport and communications
[f]Distribution in 1964

Source: UN, World Economic Survey, 1967 (New York, 1968), p. 27.

Although not approaching 30 per cent per annum,
growth rates of output in manufacturing industry
have been high in some coffee exporting countries,
as Table 8 shows.  But the methods used in manufacturing, often transferred from the advanced countries
where they were developed in conditions of labor
scarcity, tend to be labor-saving.  Moreover, where
the composition of manufacturing output shifts from
light consumer goods to heavier industrial products,
the weight of the more capital-intensive activities
in the total rises and the demand for labor tends
to be less than it would otherwise be, even if techniques in each sector are unchanged.  Even where
labor-using methods are available, they often require
management, supervision and other skills in larger
proportions than do some labor-saving methods.

The tendency to use labor-saving methods is
reinforced by minimum wage legislation and trade
union pressure for higher wages, which discourage
employers from making use of the labor even where
techniques appropriate to the employment of plentiful
cheap labor are available or where the production of
labor-intensive products would be profitable at
lower wages.

As a result the growth of employment in manufacturing is much slower than the growth of output
(see Table 9).  Substantial growth in output may
not generate <u>any</u> increase in employment as happened
in Guatemala, and may even be accompanied by a considerable decline as was the case in Kenya.

## CHOICE OF TECHNIQUE

While there can be no doubt about the urgency
of fuller labor utilization in a well-designed development strategy, the discussion is sometimes ob-
scured by two types of confusion:  is one between the
choice of labor-intensive industries and products
and the choice of labor-intensive techniques within
a given industry in producing a given product; the
other between labor-intensity in relation to capital
and in relation to output.

TABLE 8

Average Annual Percentage Rates of Growth
of Manufacturing Output

|  | 1950-60 | 1960-67 |
|---|---|---|
| Brazil[a] | 9.1 | 4.1 |
| Colombia | 6.8 | 5.5 |
| Guatemala | 4.7 | 7.9 |
| El Salvador |  | 9.7[b] |
| Ethiopia |  | 10.2[b] |
| Kenya | 7.6[d] | 5.7[e] |
| Tanzania |  | 10.6 |
| Uganda | 1.3[c] | 7.3 |

[a]Includes construction, mining, electricity, gas
  and water
[b]1960-66
[c]1954-60
[d]1954-64
[e]1964-68

Sources: El Salvador: U.N., Economic Survey
of Latin America (1968).
Kenya, 1954-64: Republic of Kenya, Development
Plan 1966-70, (Nairobi: 1966) p. 17; 1964-68:
Africa South of the Sahara (London: Europa, 1971).
Others: U.N., Yearbook of National Account
Statistics, Vol. II, (1968), Table 56.

TABLE 9

Annual Percentage Increase of Employment
In Manufacturing

| | | |
|---|---|---|
| Brazil* | 1950-60 | 2.6 |
| Colombia | 1960-67 | 0.5 |
| Guatemala | 1960-67 | negligible |
| El Salvador | 1961-67 | 3.0 |
| Kenya | 1954-64 | -1.1 |
| Tanzania | 1960-67 | 4.0 |
| Uganda | 1960-67 | 3.5 |

*Industrial employment

Sources:  Brazil:  I. Little, T. Scitovsky,
M. Scott, Industry and Trade in Some Developing Countries (London:  Oxford University Press, 1970), p.
84.
     Kenya:  Republic of Kenya, Development Plan
1966-70 (Nairobi: 1966), p. 27.
     Others:  U.N., Statistical Yearbook, (1969).


     Foreign trade apart, it is often said that there
is limited scope for permitting the composition of
industries and the product-mix to be determined by
factor availabilities.  Hair-cutting is labor-intensive, but this can be no reason for developing
countries to establish large barbering sectors.  Some
consumer goods are more labor-intensive than many
capital goods, but this can be no reason for encouraging consumption at the expense of investment.  At
the same time, there may be a good deal more scope
if one envisages new product designs to meet the
different needs of consumers in developing countries.
Many existing products, transferred from advanced
countries, satisfy a whole range of wants, some of
which are inappropriate or unnecessary for poorer

consumers.[9] More appropriate products (rather than technologies) may hold out hopes for fuller labor utilization.

Where there is scope for choosing labor-intensive products that serve the objectives decided upon, clearly these should be chosen. And having determined the sectoral structure and the product-mix, it is sensible to employ techniques, where these are available, that economize in scare factors and make fuller use of abundant factors. In some industries, there is a variety of processes between which one can choose, particularly if ancillary activities like moving goods or loading them are taken into account.

Next, it is important to avoid saving capital in relation to labor in a way that reduces output per unit of capital, unless job creation is regarded as an independent objective, for which it is worth sacrificing output. In particular, the advocates of labor-using techniques sometimes fail to pay adequate attention to the capital requirements of inventories and work-in-progress.

While it is desirable to use, _ceteris paribus_, methods of production that save capital per worker, it is not desirable to do so if this means using more capital per unit of output, i.e., reducing production by more than in proportion to the capital saved. The ratio of labor to capital is identically equal to the ratio of labor to product, divided by the capital/output ratio. An increase in the labor/capital ratio that is achieved by raising the capital/output ratio has not much to commend it.[10]

In the conditions prevailing in the coffee-producing countries, the right result cannot always be taken for granted. It is likely that so-called labor-intensive methods will show less _fixed_ capital per worker. Visible structures and equipment may be smaller. But particularly in rural and dispersed industries, requirements of working capital (inventories and work-in-progress) are likely to increase. Work-in-progress is likely to be greater, the more

dispersed the industry, the longer the distances
from the centers, the higher the wastage of material
and the greater the losses from lack of standardi-
zation of product.   Inventories are also likely to
be greater because economies of scale will not be
available in stock holding.   Investigations in India
have shown that labor-intensive methods of production
are, for these reasons, often capital-intensive in
relation to output.[11]

The argument so far has been that labor-intensive
methods should be efficient, i.e., they should not
require more labor and more capital.  In many cases
there will be little or no choice of techniques and
only capital-intensive methods will be available.
If the raw material is available locally, if other
criteria are favorable and unit costs of production
are internationally competitive, capital intensity
should not in itself stand in the way of adopting
the process.  In the long run, only accelerated
development can solve the problem of unemployment
and for this production at low costs is essential.


## NOTES

1.   Joan Robinson, "Disguised Unemployment,"
Economic Journal, Vol. XLVI, No. 182 (June 1936),
225-37, reprinted in her Essays in the Theory of
Employment (Oxford: Basil Blackwell, 1943), pp. 60-
74.

2.   A similar identity was first used in April
1961 by Michael Lipton in a working paper for Gunnar
Myrdal's Asian Drama (London:  Allen Lane, The Penguin
Press, 1968).  See also W. J. Barber, "Some Questions
about Labor Force Analysis in Agrarian Economies
with particular reference to Kenya", East African
Economic Review, Vol. 2, New Series No. 1., (June
1966), and Myrdal, op. cit.

3.   Myrdal, op. cit., p. 1072.

4.   Lauchlin Currie, Accelerating Development
(New York:  McGraw Hill, 1966), p. 168: ". . . there

is a great deal of idleness, voluntary, and involuntary [in Colombia]. In the Ivory Coast, the essence
of the primitive methods of producing coffee is
described by Professor Barna as minimizing the amount
of work necessary for obtaining a coffee crop of any
sort." (See also, Barna's contribution to the Joint
Coffee Study by the International Bank for Reconstruction and Development, the International Coffee Organization, and the FAO, Mimeographed, 1968).

5.   The distinction is due to P. Sargant
Florence, The Logic of British and American Industry
(London: Routledge and Kegan Paul, 1953). The
application to the theory of controls was suggested
by Michael Lipton to Gunnar Myrdal. Further sub-
divisions are possible by combining the general-
specific and positive-negative distinctions with
those in Table 5.

6.   Currie, op. cit. p. 156: "The relative
high productivity of the machine, and the use of
better techniques in commercial farming lower the
return the colonial-type farmer can gain and make
it even less practical for him to do all the costly
things that would increase his productivity."

7.   P. N. Rosenstein-Rodan, "Disguised Unemployment and Underemployment in Agriculture," FAO,
Monthly Bulletin of Agricultural Economics and Statistics, Vol. VI, No. 7/8, (July/August 1957), 1-7.

8.   Ibid.

9.   Frances Stewart, "Choice of Techniques"
(unpublished paper, written as part of a project
conducted at Queen Elizabeth House, Oxford, in 1970).

10.   On this whole set of problems, see Frances
Stewart and Paul Streeten, "Conflicts between Output
and Employment Objectives," Oxford Economic Papers
(July 1971).

11.   P. N. Dhar and H. F. Lydall, The Role of
Small Enterprises in Indian Economic Development
(Bombay: Asia Publishing House, 1961).

ARGO-INDUSTRIAL UNITS

It is now generally recognized that the dispute
over whether first priority should be given to agriculture or to industry is a sham dispute and that
progress in one is a condition for progress in the
other.  At the same time, the emphasis on industrialization and the success with which it was tackled
have brought out the need for faster progress in         ·
agriculture.  In many developing countries it was the
unbalanced progress in industry that brought out with ·
particular force the need to reform agriculture.
The agricultural sector dominates the economy by its
sheer size, in terms of its contribution both to gross
domestic product and to employment.  If the standard
of living of the mass of the people is to rise, then
clearly a rapid rate of agricultural growth must be
achieved.  This is all the more important in view of
the rapid rates of population growth--the annual rate
of population growth was at least 3 per cent in Colombia, El Salvador and Guatemala in the decade 1955-65,
and at least 2 per cent in Brazil, Kenya and Uganda.[1]
Moreover, agricultural stagnation can be a brake on
industrial advance (1) because only a prosperous
agriculture can supply industry with a marketable
surplus of food and raw materials at a stage when
there is no longer a need for this surplus to be
absorbed in the agricultural sector itself, (2)
because it is a source of savings for an investible
surplus wherever the highest social returns are to
be earned, though this may well be within the agricultural sector, (3) because it can earn, directly or
indirectly, foreign exchange that can be used for
scarce industrial imported inputs, (4) because a
prosperous agriculture can provide a mass market for
industrial consumer and producer goods and (5) because
it can forge links that stimulate industrial development, such as providing a base for processing industries.

It is sometimes said that agriculture provides
industry with a labor force, but in prevailing conditions in developing countries, there is an abundance
of unskilled labor in both industry and agriculture,
not a shortage.  Indeed, the labor surplus can constitute an important obstacle to development, and
the rural sector--as well as the industrial sector--
has to make a large contribution to providing employment opportunities, not labor.

A useful link between agricultural and industrial
activities can often be formed by industries processing agricultural raw materials.  Such industrial
complexes cut across the distinction agriculture versus
industry and show that disputes over where to invest
or market the surpluses are false disputes.  From
the point of view of labor utilization, it is sometimes
possible to locate them in rural areas and, where
seasonal peaks in agriculture and processing do not
coincide, to link agricultural and industrial employment.  In addition to the advantages discussed later
in this chapter, such industries can make a contribution to reducing rural underemployment.

One obvious possibility for coffee-producing
countries is the further processing of coffee, so
that they can export instant or soluble coffee rather
than green (or unroasted) coffee.  Soluble coffee
was first made in 1930 but its full importance was
not recognized until the early 1950's.  It was con-
venient and relatively inexpensive, which brought it
to a wider consuming public.  During the mid-fifties
when instant coffee was first promoted heavily it
had a 30 to 40-per cent share of the market, with
liquid coffee holding a similar share and the remainder
being held by ground coffee.  By 1969 instant coffee
commanded 80 per cent of the market, with liquid
coffee having suffered the heaviest decline in popu-
larity.[2]

Since 1965, Brazil in particular has invested
in the production of instant coffee.  American and
European processors, with the exception of the European
based Nestlé group, did not respond to incentives to
set up plants in Brazil, so the Brazilians built four

manufacturing plants themselves.  By 1970 a further
five factories were in production.  These plants are
large-scale and work solely for export markets.

As Figure 1 shows, U.S. imports of soluble coffee,
mainly from Brazil, have risen steeply in recent
years, though they are still a relatively small proportion of total U.S. production (about 14 per cent
in 1967).  More importantly, the U.S. has turned
from being a major exporter to being a net importer
of soluble coffee.  The Ivory Coast is also building
up capacity in the production of soluble coffee.

However, coffee processing is not the only and
not necessarily the most desirable alternative.  The
main concern of this chapter is with industries using
agricultural, fishery and forestry products as raw
materials.  These industries account for about half
of the total value added and almost two thirds of
the employment in manufacturing industry in the
developing countries.

FIGURE 1

U.S. Trade in Soluble Coffee,
1965-68 (Jan. - Oct.)

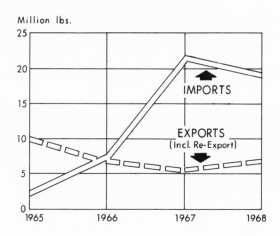

Source: The Financial Times, December 10, 1968, p. 4.

The problems that an attempt at diversification
as an integral part of a development plan has to
solve can be grouped under the general headings of
supply and demand.  For some purposes this is not an
ideal division.  Some demand limitations spring from
increased supply by rivals.  Some supply limitations
in the attitudes and responses of farmers are the
result of uncertain and fluctuating demand.  And the
whole range of problems treated under selling and
marketing and the role of middlemen do not easily
fit into a distinction between primary supplies and
final demand.  But the time-honored distinction may
serve as a starting point.


SUPPLY


Agricultural raw materials and unskilled labor,
subject to the qualifications below, may be assumed
to be in abundant supply, while capital, foreign
exchange, skills and management are scarce.  It follow
that the aim in selecting a suitable industry and
process must be to maximize returns to the scarce
factors.  Other things being equal, suitable projects
should have a low capital intensity, in the sense
that they should save capital relatively to labor
without sacrificing efficiency; should make a compara-
tively low demand on scarce types of skill, while
registering favorable repercussions on other activities in the economy; and should be conducted in com-
paratively small plants that are efficient in supply-
ing a small market.

Kenneth A. Bohr has attempted to quantify some
criteria for project identification.[3]  Assuming fairly
constant technical characteristics, he selects the
following criteria: requirements of capital and
skilled labor, plant size and locational pattern.
His findings are reproduced in Table 10.

As one would expect, some coefficients, but by
no means all, are correlated with one another.  The
more scattered industries generally operate with
smaller plants.  Industry groups with the lowest and
the highest capital requirements show the least need

for skilled labor.  Few industries have low coefficients for all the characteristics that would make
them suitable for developing countries.  Thus rubber
goods and electrical machinery show low capital
requirements but tendencies toward large-scale production, while electrical machinery, ready-made
clothing and jewelry, which also have low capital
requirements, show high requirements for skilled
labor.  On the other hand, industries with high capital
requirements have advantages in other respects.
Cement products, bricks and tiles, meat packing,
fish-curing and condensed milk have high capital
requirements but are more suitable by other criteria.
But, taking a balance of considerations, it appears
that many industries based on agricultural raw materials score high by these criteria and are suitable
for developing countries.

In addition to these characteristics, the spin-
off effects of the industry on the rest of the economy
and in particular on the traditional sector must be
considered.  A well-located processing plant may not
only add value to the raw material, but also stimulate
a number of other activities.  It can, in addition
to satisfying existing demand, create new demand for
its products; it can stimulate new supplies of raw
material; it can create demand for a range of machinery, equipment and other inputs for small repair
shops and ancillary activities; and it can encourage
the use of waste products or by-products.  What we
should wish to know, in this context, is neither the
multiplier nor the accelerator, but a collateral,
backward or forward investment coefficient, showing
the effects of one act of investment on related other
acts.  The beneficial impact of these types of linkage
have to be compared with the claim by the processing
plant on scarce factors of production.  It must be
remembered that many of these economies, because
they are poor and underdeveloped, and because human
attitudes and social institutions are not, or not
fully, adapted to economic change, have low supply
elasticities.  Responses that would be forthcoming
in more developed economies may be absent, unless
specifically planned.  In particular, the machinery
and equipment of the processing factory will absorb

TABLE 10

Coefficients of Economic Characteristics of Selected Industries

| Industry | [a]Total Fixed Capital Requirements. | [b]Machinery & Equipment Requirements | [c]Skilled Labor Requirements | [d]Degree of Localization | [e]Prevalent Size |
|---|---|---|---|---|---|
| Boots and shoes | 1 | 3 | 1 | 3 | None |
| Soap and candles | 1 | 1 | 3 | 2 | None |
| Cooperage | 1 | 2 | 3 | 2 | 2 |
| Leather goods | 1 | 1 | 1 | 2 | 2 |
| Bedding and mattresses | 1 | 1 | 4 | 1 | 1 |
| Jewelry | 1 | 1 | 4 | 4 | 2 |
| Tailoring and ready-made clothing | 1 | 1 | 4 | 2 | None |
| Paints and varnishes | 1 | 2 | 2 | 1 | 2 |
| Hosiery | 1 | 2 | 1 | 3-4 | None |
| Knitted garments | 1 | 2 | 1 | 2 | None |
| Rubber goods and tires | 1-2 | 3 | 2 | 2 | 5 |
| Brooms and brushes | 1 | 2 | 1 | 2 | 1 |
| Glass (other than bottles) | 1 | 1 | 3 | 1 | None |
| Shirts, collars and underclothing | 1 | 1 | 1 | 2 | 3 |

| | | | | | |
|---|---|---|---|---|---|
| Electrical machinery, cables and apparatus | 2-1 | 2 | 4 | 3 | 5 |
| Tanning | 2 | 2 | 1 | 2 | 2 |
| Cardboard boxes | 2 | 2 | 2 | 1 | 2 |
| Wood textiles | 2-3 | 3 | 2 | 3 | 3 |
| Furniture | 2 | 1 | 4 | 2 | 1 |
| Sawmills | 2 | 4 | 3 | 4 (R.M.) | 1 |
| Planing mills, woodturning, etc. | 2 | 1 | 3 | 2 | 1 |
| Sheet metal work | 2 | 3 | 3 | 1 | 1 |
| Nonferrous foundries | 2 | 3 | 4 | 1 | None |
| Millinery | 2 | 1 | 1 | 2 | 1 |
| Marble, slate, etc. | 2 | 3 | 4 | 3 (R.M.) | 1 |
| Cutlery and small hand tools | 2 | 3 | 3 | 3 | None |
| Fabricated plastics | 2 | 1 | 3 | 1 | None |
| Steelworks and rolling mills | 2-4 | 4 | 4 | 3 | 5 |
| Steel wire and products | 2 | 2 | 3 | 1 | None |
| Stoves, ovens, ranges | 2 | 4 | 3 | 2 | None |
| Agricultural machinery and implements | 2-3 | 3 | 4 | 4 | None |
| Iron foundries | 3 | 2 | 3 | 1 | None |
| Textile dyeing and finishing, etc. | 3 | 3 | 2 | 3 | None |

| Industry | | | | | |
|---|---|---|---|---|---|
| Earthenware, china, etc. | 3 | 2 | 1 | 4 | 3 |
| Canning, jam, fruit, vegetables | 3-2 | 3 | 2 | 3 (R.M.) | 2 |
| Tobacco | 3-1 | 2 | 1 | 3 | 4 |
| Printing, general | 3-2 | 2 | 4 | 1-2 | None |
| Cordage and twine | 3 | 3 | 2 | 2 | None |
| Breweries | 3-2 | 3 | 1 | 1 | None |
| Motor vehicle repairs | 3 | 1 | 4 | 1 | 1 |
| Cement products | 3 | 4 | 3 | 1 | 1 |
| Newspapers and periodicals | 3-2 | 2 | 4 | 1 | 2 |
| Cotton textiles | 4 | 4 | 2 | 4 | 3 |
| Meat-packing | 4-3 | 2 | 2 | 3 (R.M.) | None |
| Fish-curing | 4 | 2 | 1 | 4 (R.M.) | 1 |
| Shipbuilding | 4-1 | 3 | 4 | 3 | 4 |
| Cement | 4 | 4 | 3 | 1 | 3 |
| Vegetable oil | 4 | 4 | 2 | 4 (R.M.) | 1 |
| Chemical fertilizers | 4 | 4 | 1 | 4 | None |
| Petroleum refining | 4 | 4 | 4 | 4 | 4 |
| Tire retreading and repairing | 4 | 1 | 2 | 1 | 1 |
| Synthetic textiles | 4 | 4 | 3 | 4 | 5 |
| Glass bottles | 4 | 4 | 3 | 3 | None |

| Industry | Capital requirements[a] | Machinery and equipment requirements[b] | Skilled labor requirements[c] | Localization coefficient[d] | Prevalent size[e] |
|---|---|---|---|---|---|
| Condensed and dried milk | 4-3 | 4 | 1 | 4 (R.M.) | 1 |
| Brick and tile | 4 | 4 | 2 | 1 | 2 |
| Nonferrous rolling, etc. | 4-2 | 4 | 4 | 2 | None |
| Bakeries | 4-1 | 1 | 1 | 1 | 1-2 |
| Paper-making | 4-3 | 4 | 3 | 1 | 3 |
| Dehydrated fruit and vegetables | 4 | 3 | 2 | 3 (R.M.) | 2 |
| Industrial chemicals | 4 | 4 | 4 | 2 | 4 |
| Flour-milling | 4-2 | 3 | 4 | 3 | 1 |
| Butter | 4 | 3 | 1 | 4 (R.M.) | 1 |

Note: Numbers refer to position in a ranking of coefficients. The lower the number the lower the requirements, the more scattered the locational pattern, or the smaller the size.

[a]Capital requirements: Based on ratios of value of fixed capital to value added. Australia 1946-47. Where there are two figures, the second refers to U.S. 1939.

[b]Machinery and equipment requirements: Based on ratios of value of machinery and equipment to total value of fixed capital. Australia 1946-47.

[c]Skilled labor requirements: Based on ratio of professional persons, skilled workers and foremen to total employees. U.S. 1930.

[d]Localization coefficient: Based on geographical distribution as measured by employment. U.S. 1939. "R.M." indicates location close to sources of raw materials.

[e]Prevalent size: Based on size of median firm in cases where distribution of employment by firm size shows a regular distribution. U.K. and U.S. 1930 and 1929. In cases where size classification differed between the two countries the most favorable (the smallest) classification has been used. "None" indicates no prevalent size.

Source: Kenneth A. Bohr, "Investment Criteria for Manufacturing Industries in Underdeveloped Countries," Review of Economics and Statistics, Vol. XXXVI (May 1954), pp. 157-66.

foreign exchange and the skills exercised in setting
it up and running it will tend to be scarce.  A
balance sheet of net advantages will have to be drawn
up, showing the value added to the raw material, minus
costs of capital and skills, plus benefits of any
spread effects upon other activities in the economy.


                              DEMAND


     A forward linkage, by which one or more stages
of processing are added to the production of the raw
material, if intended for import substitution, benefits from the knowledge that a demand for the processed
product already exists.  Domestic processing replaces
processing abroad and foreign exchange is saved.
The process may initially have to be subsidized or
protected on infant industry grounds.  The problems
of efficient import substitution and the size of the
internal market are discussed further in Chapter 6.
If the processed product is intended for export, the
subsidies that it can receive are limited by international rules.  In the code of international economic
morality that has evolved since the end of World War
II and is embodied in our international economic
institutions, export subsidies are regarded with
peculiar disapproval.[4]  In the case of soluble coffee,
disagreement between Brazil and the United States
on the promotion of Brazilian industry very nearly
prevented the renewal of the International Coffee
Agreement in 1968.  The essence of the dispute was
the complaint by the U.S. industry that the Brazilian
industry was able to obtain green coffee beans at a
lower price from American processors, and thus enjoyed
an unfair advantage.  This came about because a tax
was imposed upon exports of green coffee but not
upon sales to domestic processors.  Thus the Brazilian
instant coffee industry received a de facto subsidy.
Charges of dumping soluble coffee on the American
market were made against Brazil, and the U.S. ratified
the agreement for only a further three years, instead
of the full five years.

     Under pressure from the U.S. government, Brazil
agreed in 1969 to place an export tax of 13 cents

per pound on soluble coffee.  Subsequently the U.S.
pressed for it to be increased to 30 cents per pound.
Eventually the dispute was settled in March 1971,
when Brazil agreed to ship 560,000 bags of green
coffee to U.S. soluble coffee manufacturers free of
the export tax.  There is provision for this quota
to be increased or reduced, depending on the performance of shipments of Brazilian soluble coffee to the
U.S.  In return, the U.S. agreed to the removal of
the 13 cents a pound export tax.

In export markets the new processing industry
must also face the obstacle of the present tariff
structure of advanced industrial countries, which
discriminates against processing more severely than
appears from nominal tariff rates.  Recent work on
the effective tariff has clarified this issue.  The
basic point is simple:  If an advanced country admits
a raw material duty-free, if processing constitutes
50 per cent of the final value of the product and if
a tariff of 20 per cent is imposed on the final product, the effective tariff rate on processing is 40
per cent.*  From the point of view of encouraging
processing in the developing country, it would be
preferable if the advanced country imposed a tariff
of 20 per cent both on the raw material and on the
final product.  The fact that tariff rates cascade
and tend to be higher, the greater the value added,
is a powerful deterrent to the establishment in the
developing countries of industries adding value to
the indigenous raw materials.  Some calculations of
effective tariff rates are made in Table 11.

It follows that, from the point of view of encouraging processing industries, import duties on raw
materials and protectionist policies for agricultural

---

*Suppose the finished product costs £100 and the
raw material £50, so that value added is £50.  The
import duty payable on the finished product is £20.
Then the effective tariff rate

$$= \frac{\text{duty payable on finished product}}{\text{value added}} = \frac{£20}{£50} = 40\%$$

TABLE 11

Tariff Rates For Selected Agricultural Products in Raw and
Processed Form in Main Industrial Countries, 1963

| | EEC[a] | | United Kingdom | | United States | |
|---|---|---|---|---|---|---|
| | Nom.[b] | Effec.[c] | Nom.[b] | Effec.[c] | Nom.[b] | Effec.[c] |
| | | | | (Per cent) | | |
| WOOD & WOOD PRODUCTS | | | | | | |
| 1. Wood in the rough & roughly squared (SITC 242)[d] | - | ... | - | ... | - | ... |
| 2. Veneer & plywood (SITC 631) | 10 | ... | 10 | ... | 16.8 | 37.9 |
| 3. Wood products, including furniture (SITC 632) | 15.1 | 28.6 | 14.8 | 25.5 | 12.8 | 26.4 |
| LEATHER & LEATHER PRODUCTS | | | | | | |
| 1. Hides & skins, undressed (SITC 211) | - | ... | - | ... | - | ... |
| 2. Leather (SITC 611) | 7.3 | 18.3 | 14.9 | 34.3 | 9.6 | 25.7 |
| 3. Leather manufactures, (SITC 612) Shoes | 19.9 | 33.0 | 24.0 | 36.2 | 16.6 | 25.3 |
| Leather manufactures other than shoes | 14.7 | 24.3 | 18.7 | 26.4 | 15.5 | 24.5 |
| WOOL & WOOL PRODUCTS | | | | | | |
| 1. Wool & animal hair (SITC 262) | - | ... | 0-10 | ... | 0-47 | ... |
| 2. Yarn of wool & animal hair (SITC 651.2) | 8 | ... | 17 | ... | 25 | ... |
| 3. Woven wool fabrics (SITC 653.2) | 18 | ... | 22 | ... | 46 | ... |
| RUBBER & RUBBER PRODUCTS | | | | | | |
| 1. Rubber, natural (SITC 231.1) | - | ... | - | ... | - | ... |
| 2. Rubber tires and tubes (SITC 629.1) | 20 | ... | 27 | ... | 19 | ... |

COCOA & COCOA PRODUCTS

| | | | | | | |
|---|---|---|---|---|---|---|
| 1. Cocoa beans, raw (SITC 072.1) | 5.4 | ... | 1.5 | ... | - | ... |
| 2. Cocoa powder & cocoa butter, (SITC 072.2 and 072.3) | 20-27 | 136 | 0.5-2.0 | 13 | 6.5 | 50 |

COTTON & COTTON PRODUCTS

| | | | | | | |
|---|---|---|---|---|---|---|
| 1. Cotton, raw (SITC 263.1) | - | ... | - | ... | - | ... |
| 2. Cotton yarn and thread (SITC 651.4) | 2.9 | 3.6 | 10.5 | 27.9 | 11.7 | 31.8 |
| 3. Cotton fabrics (SITC 652.1 and 652.2) | 17.6 | 44.4 | 20.7 | 42.2 | 24.1 | 50.6 |
| 4. Clothing (except fur clothing)e (SITC 841) | 18.5 | 25.1 | 25.5 | 40.5 | 25.1 | 35.9 |

Note:    SITC = Standard International Trade Classification
    ... = Does not apply
    - = No tariff

aCommon External Tariff.

bTariff rates as actually applied to the specified product.

cCalculated rate of protection accorded to value added in the manufacturing process.

dStage of processing.

eClothing manufactured from any fibre.

Source:  UNCTAD, "Tariff structures of selected developed countries and their effect on export of processed goods from developing countries," Document TD/B/C.2/9, February 7, 1966 (mimeo), pp. 4-6.

products generally in advanced countries are less objectionable than the cascading tariff rates on processed materials.*  From a policy point of view, this argument implies that industrializing developing countries should give higher priority to the reduction of high effective tariffs that impede processing in developing countries than to the reduction of agricultural protection in advanced countries.[5]  The argument is strengthened if it is recalled that agriculture is subject to diminishing returns, industrial processing to increasing returns.

Tariffs are not the only obstacle to increased trade in processed products from developing countries. There are also other forms of trade restrictions, some of them more powerful, and there are difficulties of marketing for newcomers.

An UNCTAD study attempts to identify the dynamic items imported by the developed market economies from the developing countries.[6]  The report finds that, excluding petroleum products and base metals, there is a high concentration in a few groups both of amounts and of rates of growth between 1955 and 1965.  In 1965 nearly 75 per cent of total imports of manufactures from the developing countries were concentrated on 19 main products.  These accounted for nearly 18 per cent of the developed countries' total imports of the products in question, while total imports from the developing countries were only a little over 5 per cent of developed countries' imports.  The tendency toward concentration increased between 1955 and 1965.  Whereas the share of imports from developing countries in the developed countries' total imports declined slightly (from 6 per cent in 1955 to 5.2 per cent in 1965), the share of the 19 principal manufactures showed an increase (from 15.9 per cent in 1955 to 17.7 per cent in 1965).  These 19 main products are listed in Table 12.

---------------

*If tariff rates on raw materials exceeded the rate on the finished product, the effective tariff would be negative and would constitute a form of subsidy to processing abroad.

TABLE 12

Product Groups Imported from Developing Countries in Substantial
Amounts, 1965

| | | Value of Imports, 1965 ($ million) |
|---|---|---|
| 1. | Clothing | 432 |
| 2. | Fabrics (other than cotton) | 252 |
| 3. | Shaped wood | 216 |
| 4. | Alcoholic beverages | 200 |
| 5. | Cotton fabrics | 194 |
| 6. | Fruit, preserved and fruit preparations | 154 |
| 7. | Prepared or preserved meat | 143 |
| 8. | Floor coverings | 138 |
| 9. | Plywood and veneers | 118 |
| 10. | Leather products | 97 |
| 11. | Textile products (n.e.s.)* | 91 |
| 12. | Manufactured articles (n.e.s.)* | 91 |
| 13. | Inorganic chemicals | 86 |
| 14. | Prepared or preserved vegetables | 78 |
| 15. | Pig-iron, etc. | 65 |
| 16. | Perambulators and toys | 65 |
| 17. | Prepared or preserved fish | 62 |
| 18. | Textile yarn and thread | 56 |
| 19. | Essential oils and perfumes | 53 |

* n.e.s. = not elsewhere specified

Source: UNCTAD, "Dynamic Products in Developing Countries' Exports of Manufactures
and Semi-Manufactures," Document TB/B/C.2/47, October 27, 1967.

It will be seen that these exports consist
mainly of products that can be produced with simple
techniques and/or require processing of local raw
materials.  While the share of these items in the
total imports of developed countries is falling,
their share in developing countries' exports and in
the imports of developed from developing countries
is rising.

The report also identifies the products with
very high growth rates in imports from the developing
countries, distinguishing between traditional and
new products.  The list largely overlaps with that
of the 19 principal exports, confirming the tendency
toward concentration in simple technology and/or
processed products.

If, among the imports from developing countries
showing a high growth rate, we select those that can
be regarded as traditional imports (the import values
of each which amounted in 1955 to at least $10 mil-
lion), we find that during the period 1955-65, 12
product groups had annual growth rates above the
median growth rate for imports as a whole.  These
products are listed in decreasing order of growth
rate in Table 13.

The largest increase in imports of processed
food products from developing countries was in the
category of preserved fruit and fruit preparations,
in which the annual rate of growth for 1955-65 was
11.7 per cent.  Wood pulp, plywood and veneers, foot-
wear, leather goods and vegetable preparations also
showed dynamism.  The UNCTAD report concludes that
a tendency toward an international division of
labor can be discerned, the developed countries
trading largely and increasingly with each other in
the products of a sophisticated technology, while
the share of developing countries in simpler manufactures, often based on processing of natural
resources, is rising.

Trade in these simpler manufactures is, however,
largely confined to a few less-developed countries.
In 1965 only 14 countries had a share of the market

TABLE 13

Growth in Traditional Imports from Developing Countries, 1955-65

| | Average Annual Growth Rate, 1955-65 (%) |
|---|---|
| 1. Clothing | 28.8 |
| 2. Plywood and veneers | 21.0 |
| 3. Miscellaneous manufactured articles | 19.7 |
| 4. Cotton fabrics | 18.5 |
| 5. Textile products (n.e.s.)* | 18.2 |
| 6. Floor coverings and tapestries | 14.5 |
| 7. Footwear | 12.5 |
| 8. Textile yarn and thread | 12.2 |
| 9. Fruit preparations | 11.7 |
| 10. Inorganic chemicals | 10.9 |
| 11. Silver and platinum | 10.8 |
| 12. Vegetable preparations | 10.7 |

*n.e.s. = not elsewhere specified

Source: UNCTAD, "Dynamic Products in Developing Countries' Exports of Manufactures and Semi-Manufactures," Document TB/B/C.2/47, October 27, 1967.

amounting to 2 per cent or more, and these 14 accounted between them for nearly 75 per cent of the
total market (see Table 14).

Of the major coffee countries only Mexico and
Brazil are important in this context.  Brazil's
manufactured exports are mainly processed foodstuffs,
shaped wood and chemicals.  Mexico also exports
chemicals and foodstuffs, plus nonferrous wrought

TABLE 14

Imports of Manufactures and Semi-Manufactures
into Developed Market-Economy Countries
from Developing Countries,
By Main Countries of Origin, 1965

|  | Percentage Distribution |
|---|---|
| Hong Kong | 20.2 |
| India | 13.2 |
| Yugoslavia | 7.1 |
| Mexico | 5.0 |
| Algeria | 4.5 |
| Taiwan | 4.1 |
| Brazil | 3.6 |
| Argentina | 2.8 |
| Iran | 2.8 |
| Israel | 2.7 |
| Malaysia/Singapore | 2.4 |
| Philippines | 2.4 |
| Morocco | 2.0 |
| Pakistan | 2.0 |
| Others | 25.2 |
| TOTAL | 100.0 |

Source: UNCTAD, Proceedings of United Nations
Conference on Trade and Development, Second Session,
Vol. III, "Review of the Trade in Manufactures and
Semi-Manufactures:  Report by the UNCTAD Secretariat,
(TD/10/Supp. 1, Table 6) pp. 125-48.

metals (such as silver).  The Ivory Coast has begun
to develop processing industries and along with
Mexico was responsible for large increases in exports
of preserved fruit and fruit preparations.

It is not altogether easy to derive clear lessons
from these findings.  For one thing, although many
of the dynamic products are being produced labor-
intensively, some of them are capital-intensive.
However, supply considerations also suggest that
capital intensity, where choice of technique is
limited, should not stand in the way of producing
products for which the demand is rapidly expanding
and for which a raw material base exists in the
country.  In any case, as we have seen in Chapter 3,
the division of factors into labor and capital is
far too crude to provide guidance.  Capital- (i.e.
fixed capital) intensive processes may economize
in other even scarcer factors, such as skills or
foreign exchange.

Moreover, while the success--both in terms of
shares and of growth rates--of certain technically
simple and processed items in the developing countries'
export performance may point toward further concentration on these and similar items, it must be
remembered that although a small share of the market
may be a promising base for an increase, it is also
subject to the threat of substantial contraction if
large rival firms take retaliatory action.  Success
may be easy while the amounts involved are small
but this does not ensure that progress will be
equally easy beyond a certain threshold, when the
established rivals begin to take notice.  When
Brazil was exporting only $743,000-worth of instant
coffee (in 1965) American rivals were not particularly
worried; but two years later when exports had leapt
to $28.262 million, the U.S. National Coffee Associ-
ation began to lobby for retaliatory measures.

There is, it is true, the possibility of exporting
manufactures and semi-manufactures to the Socialist
countries of Eastern Europe.  Such exports have
grown rapidly:  Negligible in 1935, they rose to
around $200 million by 1961 and to $558 million by

1965.[7]  However, this is still not a very high absolute
level; the EEC countries in 1965 imported $1,094 mil-
lion-worth of manufactures and semimanufactures from
less-developed countries.  The Eastern European countries in fact accounted for only about 13½ per cent of
such imports from less-developed countries to the rest
of the world.  Moreover, of the $558 million, just
over 60 per cent comes from Yugoslavia alone; the addition of India and the United Arab Republic would seem
to account for about another 30 per cent of the total.
The bulk of the items imported from less-developed
countries other than Yugoslavia were textile goods,
although there are now increasing efforts to diversify
trade.

An interesting new idea being pursued by Brazil
is to export instant coffee factories.  The Brazilian
Coffee Institute is financing the installation of a
soluble coffee plant in the Soviet Union which is
expected to absorb 500,000 bags of Brazilian coffee a
year.[8]

Apart from selling to the Eastern European countries, the answer lies perhaps in the maintenance of
high levels of demand and high rates of growth.
Against the dangers from faster technical progress
of the advanced countries--i.e., an acceleration in
the growth of synthetics, in economy in raw material
input and in the shift toward low-import-content com-
modities--high demand and high growth stimulate the
search for imports of labor-intensive commodities
and facilitate the occupational shifts in advanced
countries that free access to their markets, combined
with full employment, require.  The encouragement of
imports of labor-intensive processes and commodities
springs from the fact that technical progress tends
to raise real wages in advanced countries, where the
labor force grows only slowly.[9]  Since labor does
not move readily from poor to rich countries, it
becomes profitable to establish factories in the
poor countries, where cheap labor can be combined
with capital and know-how from the rich countries.
This process is assisted by the fact that the poor
countries acquire a comparative advantage in training labor, the cost of which is partly the foregone
earnings of the trainers.  And these are higher in

the rich countries as a result of technical progress, high rates of growth and high levels of demand.

Recent trends in world demand are not too encouraging.[10] World production in 1970 rose by little more than 3 per cent, the lowest figure since 1958. In turn world trade suffered; in terms of volume there was a 7-per cent rise, but this was 1 per cent below the average of the past ten years. Some comfort, however, may be derived from the fact that in relation to world output, trade increased more rapidly than in any of the previous postwar slowdowns.

The other part of the answer lies in the removal of trade restrictions and in an agreement on an international code of behavior, which would prevent advanced countries from imposing additional import restrictions whenever strong pressure is exercised by vested interests, particularly since better access to low-cost goods is as much in the general interest of the importing as in that of the exporting countries. The UNCTAD Generalized Preference Scheme, agreed in October 1970, for certain manufactured and processed exports from less-developed countries may help.[11] All the preference-granting countries have reserved the right to limit or withdraw any of the concessions if they consider it necessary to protect their domestic interests.

NOTES

1. U.N., World Economic Survey, 1967 (New York: 1968), p. 36.

2. The London Times, "Coffee: A Special Report," March 27, 1969, p. 1.

3. Kenneth A. Bohr, "Investment Criteria for Manufacturing Industries in Underdeveloped Countries," Review of Economics and Statistics, Vol. XXXVI (May 1954), pp. 157-66.

4. See Paul Streeten, "The Case for Export Subsidies," The Journal of Development Studies, Vol. V (July 1969), pp. 270-73.

5.  See FAO, International Commodity Arrangements and Policies, Commodity Policy Studies, p. 47.
It is shown there that, while lessening agricultural
protection would affect 30 per cent of underdeveloped
countries' exports of primary products, reducing the
differential tariff for raw and processed goods
would affect 80 per cent.

6.  UNCTAD, "Dynamic Products in Developing
Countries' Exports of Manufactures and Semi-Manufactures," Document TB/B/C.2/47, October 27, 1967.

7.  UNCTAD, Proceedings of United Nations Con-
ference on Trade and Development, Second Session,
Vol. III, "Review of the Trade in Manufactures and
Semi-Manufactures:  Report by the UNCTAD Secretariat,"
(TD/10/Supp.1, Table 6) pp. 125-48.

8.  The Financial Times, August 13, 1969, p.4.

9.  Harry G. Johnson, Economic Policies Toward
Less Developed Countries, (London: Allen & Unwin,
1967), p. 50.

10.  Secretariat of the General Agreement on
Tariffs and Trade, as reported in The Financial Times,
February 16, 1971.

11.  UNCTAD "Report of the Trade and Development
Board In Its Fourth Special Session," Document
TD/B/330, October 14, 1970.

# 5

## A PROPOSAL FOR JOINT VENTURES

The formation of units that can process domestic raw materials requires capital, management, know-how, technical skills and foreign exchange. These are scarce. A country embarking on such enterprises is faced with a dilemma. Should it invite foreign firms that bring with them a package of these scarce resources but who also have potential drawbacks? Or should it try to "go it alone?"

Foreign firms may demand high profits and government concessions such as tax holidays, protection against competitors, import licences, etc. It is true that from their point of view foreign investment may be thought particularly risky. The fear of expropriation without prompt and adequate compensation, or of restrictions on profit remittances adds to the political risks and raises the rate of return required by foreign companies before they invest. The fact that expropriations and interferences with remittances are not very common does not necessarily eliminate or reduce the subjective fear in the minds of investors. Actions taken by one country affect the returns required from investment in others, which have no intention of taking similar actions. In any case, the monopolistic powers that foreign enterprises enjoy often enable them to remit abroad, in one way or another, a large part of the value added by the enterprise. On the other hand, it is often argued that as long as foreign investment raises production, and this increase is not wholly appropriated by the investor, the greater product must be shared with others in the host country. It could accrue to domestic labor as higher real wages, or to consumers by way of lower prices, or to the government as tax revenue. There could be indirect gains through the realization of other external economies.

Nevertheless, the danger exists that these industrial activities remain foreign enclaves without
spreading their benefits over the indigenous sector,
or, worse, that they damage indigenous efforts.  If
the product is mainly for export, then any benfit in
the form of lower prices will accrue mainly to foreign
consumers.  If the firm is vertically integrated to
a large degree, then most pecuniary external economies
will be internalized rather than stimulate additional
domestic investment.[1]  The impact on the quality of
the domestic labor force depends upon the training
and recruiting policies pursued by the foreign firm.
What may happen is that the foreign firm creates a
small group of privileged workers (at least in contrast with the bulk of the population) while retarding
the growth of indigenous managerial and entrepreneurial
abilities.[2]  To the extent that there are linkages
with outside activities it may be argued that foreign
capital will have two opposing effects on domestic
entrepreneurship:  It may encourage domestic entrepreneurs engaged in complementary and ancillary activities, while eliminating domestic actual and potential
entrepreneurs engaged in competitive activities.
However, in some Latin American and African countries
even the linked activities have frequently been under-
taken not by indigenous capitalists, but by immi-
grants.[3]  At the worst a whole potential entrepreneurial and managerial class may be converted into
rentiers and administrators.[4]

On the other hand, without some foreign participation, it may be difficult or impossible to get the
agro-industrial unit started.  The necessary talent
is not available locally, the managerial ability is
scarce, know-how is absent and hard to acquire, capital
is expensive and rationed and so on.  The task is to
invent the modern, orderly equivalent to the more
cataclysmic methods of transfer to local ownership--
liquidations and expropriations in wars, default and
bankrupticies in depressions--common in the nineteenth
century and until the last war.  We must find ways of
easing this transfer in an age when national default
on debts is rarely permitted and when anonymous transfer through local purchases of foreign bonds no longer
plays an important part, because of the dominance of
direct foreign investment.

A possible solution would be for a private firm to establish a joint enterprise with a local government or a government agency, such as a local development corporation. The foreign firm, which may already operate a plantation or an estate, should put up not more than 49 per cent of the capital, but enough to benefit if the enterprise succeeds, and of course suffer if it fails. It should have a substantial minority interest, while the local government or agency has the dominant interest.

Such a holding would often be sufficient to secure a decisive role in management. But it might be possible to arrange in special circumstances that, in the initial phase, the foreign investor should hold a higher percentage of the equity, as long as the arrangement for eventual transfer to local ownership is clearly stated. The foreign firm might also provide some of the money on a fixed interest basis or in the form of preference shares.

The equity interest of the foreign firm would be bought out by the local government at the end of a prearranged period. This period could be ten years, with provision each year, after say seven years, to extend for a further five years up to say fifteen years or longer in the case of plantation enterprises. Other forms of rolling extensions could be devised, such as periodic reviews with stated periods of extension. Alternatively, the period might be longer, but there could be options at fixed points when either the local government can buy out or the firm can sell out. An evaluation procedure to determine the price would have to be agreed.

Managerial and technical staff initially would be provided almost exclusively by the foreign firm, perhaps under a management contract, but with the obligation to train local replacements within the specified period before buy-out. The rate of replacement could not be specified contractually, but the local government would be able to use its representation on the board to ensure that it went forward at a satisfactory pace.

Housing and other community services should be provided by the local government or appropriate local statutory body set up for the purpose.  In view of the relatively short period of ownership participation, the foreign firms' capital should be concentrated on directly productive activities.

Official aid may provide the finance for partic- ipation of the local government.  It might be pos- sible to provide a long-term loan on soft terms to enable a host government to participate in a venture. No subsidy to a particular private firm would be involved, for the government's terms of on-lending could be commercial.  Only the secondary foreign exchange burden would be lightened by the soft terms. Governments can also support such joint ventures with buying-out options either by investment gurantees or by including a clause in the contract of the loan that in case of appropriation without proper compen- sation the whole outstanding loan would fall due for repayment immediately.  The force of such a clause would lie in the fear of loss of credit standing if default occurred.

Arrangements of the kind sketched out above would attract foreign capital and know-how to the activities where they are most useful, but would release them, when the host government buys out the firm, for new ventures elsewhere.  Thus good use would be made of the finance and experience of foreign companies by keeping them in a revolving fund.  Teams could be kept working together and political friction and transfer burdens would be minimized.  The company would be assured that no premature expropriation would take place and could therefore moderate its profit requirements, while the host country could forego expropriation or restrictions of remittances, because profits would be modest.  The capital set free by local purchases would be encouraged to seek new outlets in the same country.  But even if repa- triation were necessary for the capital bought out, there is now much evidence that shortage of capital has not been the main bottleneck in many developing countries and that the advantages to be gained from a transfer to local ownership and control and the encouragement to the growth of indigenous enterprise outweigh the drawbacks of having to repatriate capital.

The climate for international investment and for new forms of joint ventures would be greatly improved if a set of rules for the remittance of profits, capital and capital gains could be agreed upon and obeyed. It is important that profits earned by foreign capital should be allowed to be remitted home. Restrictions, except those imposed temporarily in emergencies, would only discourage the future flow of investment, and are as much against the interests of the investor as they are against those of the host country. But if the foreign firm borrows local capital, which it can often do very cheaply in view of its good credit standing, profits earned on this local capital need not enjoy the same freedom. The same rules should apply to these profits as those which apply to local firms.

The objectives of the proposal are, (1) to reduce the political tensions that arise from large foreign-owned enclaves in developing countries and the fears of expropriation which deter foreign enterprise; (2) to change the policies of foreign companies so that they do not necessarily subordinate the policies of the local companies to the interests of the parent companies; (3) to induce spread effects, so that the beneficial activities of the foreign companies spill over the less-dynamic sectors of the rest of the economy; (4) to set free, after a period, the scarce foreign capital and know-how so that these can be re-employed in pioneering new ventures rather than continuing to be employed in existing activities.

## NOTES

1. Pecuniary external economies arise when investment in one activity increases the profitability of other activities, for instance by reducing costs or creating demand. See T. Scitovsky, "Two Concepts of External Economies," Journal of Political Economy, Vol. LXII (April 1954) pp. 143-51.

2.   For example the workers in the Chilean copper
mines, which were American owned prior to nationali-
zation in 1964, received incomes roughly five times
higher than those of other industrial workers in the
country.   Keith Griffin, Underdevelopment in Spanish
America (London:   Allen and Unwin, 1969), p. 70.

3.   According to surveys sponsored by the UN Economic
Commission for Latin America, nearly 30 per cent of
the "empresarios" in Argentina, 41 per cent in Colombia
and 48 per cent in Chile were born abroad. See Griffin,
ibid., p. 57.

4.   In Central America this process has already
advanced very far.   See Alliance for Progress, Com-
mittee of Nine, Informe Sobre los Planes Nacionales
de Desarrollo y el Progreso de Integracion Economica
de Centro America (Washington, 1966), pp. 32, 115-16.

# 6

## FOREIGN EXCHANGE POLICY
## AND DIVERSIFICATION

The building up of alternative capacity normally requires, in the early stages, a larger volume of imports than were required for a coffee-producing economy.

There are several reasons for this hump.  Even where the alternative activity replaces some imports, or contributes to exports, it raises the demand for other imports, partly because investment in the new activities is likely to require more imported machinery and equipment than was needed in coffee growing, partly because additional maintenance imports in the form of raw materials, semifinished products, fuel, spares and components will be needed after this new capacity has come into operation and partly because some of the additional incomes generated and not fully taxed away will be spent on imports.[1]

The problem of maintenance imports is most severe when the alternative activity takes the form of establishing industries that assemble parts and components and turn out finished consumer goods, such as cars and electrical goods.  It is not likely to be so pressing when the alternative activity consists of processing indigenous agricultural raw materials. The problem of additional consumer demand could, in theory, after a time be overcome if the alternative activities take the form of producing those goods on which those who produce them, as a group, spend their additional incomes.  This includes inputs and capital goods required to produce these additional products.  A large proportion of the additional demand, but not all of it, will be for food.  But any imbalance between the production of the alternative activity and the demand generated by it will, given the prevalent downward rigidity of prices and wages,

tend to lead to inflation and additional imports.
For these reasons, the foreign exchange requirements
for building up and using alternative capacity can
then not be met fully out of the export earnings of
coffee, even if these are maintained in the face of
limiting production.


## NEED FOR FOREIGN EXCHANGE RESERVES

This has several consequences.  One is a greater
need for foreign exchange reserves.  A country holds
reserves of foreign exchange partly in order to meet
temporary deficits in its balance of payments and
partly to ease the process of adjustment where a
fundamental disequilibrium has to be corrected.
Since reserves yield no or only small monetary returns,
it is sometimes thought that developing countries
cannot afford to forego the high returns of developmental expenditure and that it is only natural, in
the light of their priorities, that they find themselves regularly short of reserves.  But this argument,
while emphasizing the high priority that must be
attached to development expenditure, neglects the
equally high or even higher damage that foreign
exchange shortages can inflict on a developing country.
The disruption of a development program and the underutilization of industrial capacity resulting from
import restrictions on raw materials, semifinished
goods, fuel, components and spare parts, the creation
of unemployment, the slowing down of the rate of
growth of production, or the conditions that may have
to be accepted in order to raise international emer-
gency loans, can inflict damage amounting to a multiple
of the returns foregone by holding a more adequate
level of reserves.

The need for reserves, expressed as a ratio of
imports, is in any case greater for developing countries than for advanced industrial countries.  This
is so for a number of reasons.  First, their export
earnings are less stable and, in the absence of large
equilibrating flows of capital, their capacity to
import is subject to large fluctuations.  Evidence
for the extreme volatility of import capacity for
five coffee-producing countries for the period 1953-

TABLE 15

Annual Rate of Growth of Capacity to Import* of Some
Coffee-Producing Countries 1954-63
(per cent)

| | Ethiopia | Brazil | Colombia | Costa Rico | Mexico |
|---|---|---|---|---|---|
| 1954 | 4.3 | 46.7 | 24.6 | 14.3 | 23.0 |
| 1955 | 1.4 | -4.0 | -30.6 | 13.8 | 36.5 |
| 1956 | -17.8 | 13.0 | 75.4 | -19.8 | -2.1 |
| 1957 | 23.3 | -6.4 | -50.1 | 15.1 | -12.5 |
| 1958 | 1.4 | -8.3 | -11.1 | 8.3 | 3.2 |
| 1959 | -8.0 | -7.3 | 30.4 | -7.7 | -10.6 |
| 1960 | 14.5 | -14.9 | -12.0 | 4.8 | 3.3 |
| 1961 | 3.8 | 46.3 | -12.4 | 5.7 | 16.3 |
| 1962 | 22.0 | -14.1 | 6.2 | 32.5 | 5.2 |
| 1963 | 0.0 | 10.2 | 10.2 | 6.4 | 0.4 |

*Import purchasing power of total net foreign exchange receipts at 1960 prices.

Source: David Wall, "Import Capacity and Economic Growth" (unpublished manuscript), 1966.

81

63 is provided by David Wall's calculations (see Table 15).

Secondly, all the coffee-producing countries except Brazil are, by any measure of size, smaller than the majority of advanced countries and there are substantial economies of scale in reserve holding of any other stocks. One would therefore expect them to require a higher ratio of reserves to imports, even if all other things were equal. Thirdly, they tend to have less access to international credit than wealthier and more experienced countries with better standing in the international capital market.

But the main reason, which is of interest in the present context (why their need for reserves in relation to imports is greater), is that the adjustment process to balance-of-payments disequilibria is slower, more painful and more costly. This, in turn, is so because they are more specialized. A diversified economy, engaging in a wide variety of activities (some of which give rise to international trade, while others meet directly domestic needs), can adjust more rapidly and more cheaply to unfavorable international changes. With factors of production specific in the short and medium long-run and exports heavily con- centrated on one or a few products, internal adjust- ments take time and cost money. In addition to the need for financing alternative activities, the country therefore will need a larger stock of foreign exchange reserves to tide itself over the period of adjustment.

Against this it is often argued that, although the need of nondiversified primary exporters for international liquid reserves may be greater than that of more diversified economies, there is no point in providing them with those reserves because they are not capable of using them as reserves should be used. Instead of using them to tide them over the adjustment process, they will use them in order to postpone or, it is argued, avoid altogether, the adjustment. In reply to this it can be said first, that such use of reserves is by no means confined to developing countries and second, that the statisti- cal evidence does not confirm the view that developing countries always run down their reserves below the

minimum level.  The reserves of the developed countries
have generally remained within the range of 30-60
per cent of their annual imports over long periods.[2]
The reserves of the less-developed countries as a
percentage of annual imports fell from a level of
more than 60 per cent in the early fifties to 40 per
cent by the mid-sixties.  However, it is helpful to
divide developing countries into three groups: oil
producers, those with initially (1951) high reserves
and the rest.  The figures show that not only the
first but also the third group, which includes the
coffee-exporting countries, maintained their ratio
of reserves to imports between 1951 and 1965 and
that while some countries permitted them to run down
too much, many properly spent excess reserves accumulated during the Korean commodity boom.  The reserve
holdings of some Latin American coffee producers are
shown in Table 16.  On the average they fall within
the 30 to 60-per cent range maintained by developed
countries.*

Therefore, it may be granted that there is, in
the early states, a hump in capital and foreign
exchange requirements for diversification; but it
then may be said that this constitutes an argument
for providing development finance, not foreign
exchange reserves.  A note of caution must be sounded
about the common method of calculating foreign aid
requirements for a developing country.  This is
to set a target rate of growth, taking into account
limitations set by the design and execution of feasible
projects, by local organizational, administrative
and technical skills, etc., to calculate the propensity
to import from past trends, making allowance for
the dual effects of any increased import substitution,
and to project likely export earnings from traditional
exports and from the growth of modern exports, allowing
for changes in prices and volumes.  To this can be
added probable receipts of private capital.  It is
then possible to derive the foreign exchange gap as
the difference between these calculated foreign exchange requirements and projected earnings, and to
regard this as a measure of the official aid required.

---

*The averages are:  Brazil 33.6 per cent;
Colombia 30.6 per cent; El Salvador 39.6 per cent;
Guatemala 42.6 per cent.

TABLE 16

Reserve Holdings as a Percentage of Imports,[a] 1951-65

| | Brazil | Colombia | El Salvador | Guatemala | Total Less-Developed Countries | Total Developed Countries |
|---|---|---|---|---|---|---|
| 1951 | 26 | 33 | 70 | 51 | 64 | 68 |
| 1952 | 26 | 40 | 65 | 58 | 60 | 71 |
| 1953 | 46 | 37 | 61 | 53 | 72 | 75 |
| 1954 | 30 | 38 | 52 | 47 | 66 | 75 |
| 1955 | 38 | 20 | 42 | 53 | 64 | 67 |
| 1956 | 50 | 20 | 37 | 51 | 61 | 62 |
| 1957 | 32 | 30 | 37 | 51 | 47 | 59 |
| 1958 | 34 | 40 | 37 | 33 | 46 | 66 |
| 1959 | 27 | 52 | 38 | 33 | 50 | 60 |
| 1960 | 24 | 34 | 27 | 39 | 44 | 57 |
| 1961 | 32 | 27 | 22 | 41 | 41 | 57 |
| 1962 | 26 | 18 | 21 | 35 | 39 | 54 |
| 1963 | 21 | 21 | 29 | 34 | 43 | 51 |
| 1964 | 29 | 21 | 28 | 30 | 40 | 47 |
| 1965[b] | 63 | 29 | 28 | 31 | 42 | 43 |

[a]Gold and foreign exchange holdings plus reserve position in the International Monetary Fund at end of year related to imports during the year.

[b]Estimate.

Source: International Monetary Fund, <u>Annual Report</u> (1966).

A difficulty of this method is that the development impact of foreign exchange is not the same, irrespective of how it accrues.  In the first place, earnings from trade, accruing to producers and traders, will be disposed of differently from loans or grants accruing to the government.  A part of the former will be taxed, but taxes will have effects on incentives and the allocation of resources. Secondly, export earnings will be matched by domestic production and incomes, part of which will be taxed, part saved and part spent on goods and services, including imports.  Receipts of official aid, on the other hand, will not be matched by such domestic counterpart flows.  A third difficulty is the assumption of a given import function, linking rigidly, though not necessarily by a constant coefficient, national income and its growth to imports.  Although structural rigidities reduce the possibility of using price adjustments to alter the demand for imports for any given level, to ignore prices and other parameters influencing demand and supply is going too far.  It is by no means safe to assume that imports of capital goods always contribute to growth and, if they cannot be produced at home, are evidence of developmental expenditure.  When imports of luxury consumer goods are restricted, imported capital goods can be used to construct domestic capacity to produce luxury goods.  On the other hand, imported food can be used to supplement domestic food to raise the surplus available to feed workers engaged in domestic capital construction, quite apart from adding to the vigor and strength of the labor force, in some countries.  The physical characteristics of imports are not a safe guide to their "essentiality" or to their contribution to overcoming structural imbalances. It is therefore advisable to use gap calculations with great caution.

In spite of these difficulties, it is possible to build up from carefully assembled local knowledge about projects, administration and available skills an optimum feasible development program and to infer from it, within broad limits, what the likely requirements of foreign exchange and foreign skills would be.  If then the micro-economic results, built up from pieces of specific knowledge, are compared with

more aggregated calculations, discrepancies may point
to relevant and fruitful questions.  But a meaningful
answer would have to distinguish between capital aid
and technical assistance and between the directions,
quality, terms and conditions of capital, rather than
to aggregate these heterogeneous components into a
single figure.


## DISADVANTAGES OF PROTECTION

The tendency for diversification to require
higher rather than lower foreign exchange expenditure
will be aggravated and prolonged if the new activities
are encouraged by protective devices that raise costs
and discourage efficiency.  If the new processed and
manufactured goods can be produced competitively and
do not require special encouragement, this difficulty
does not arise.  But frequently they will be initially,
or perhaps for a long time, produced at the high costs
of an infant industry.

Cost ratios between manufacturing and agricultural
production will be less favorable than they will be
after economies of scale have been established and
attitudes and aptitudes created.  The infant-industry
argument, often interpreted to justify protection,
is really an argument for subsidies to domestic production or factor use.  Although both protection and
subsidies tend to bring nearer together the price
ratio between manufactures and primary products and
their cost ratio, protection does it by raising the
prices of manufactures, while subsidies do it by
lowering their costs.  The argument that rural unemployment and underemployment make social costs in
manufacturing less than private costs is, in the
first instance, an argument for subsidizing wages.
The second-best solution is to subsidize manufactured
products and only the third best is to protect them.

If protective devices are adopted in an attempt
to bring internal price ratios in line with internal
cost ratios, the size of the market will be restricted.
Domestic consumers will have to pay higher prices,
and total domestic demand will be smaller.  Unless
the size of the internal market is sufficiently large

to enable productivity to rise to the point at which
costs become sufficiently low to be competitive at
world prices, the "infants" will never be able to
grow up and will always require protection.  Neither
will export capacity be increased, since production
of the processed goods will be conducted at too high
a cost to be competitive with the established processing industries of advanced industrial countries.
In addition, protection for new activities implies
discrimination against already existing activities.
For instance protection of industry, by raising the
prices that the agricultural sector pays for industrial products, amounts to a taxation of agriculture
for the benefit of industry in much the same way as
if a direct levy had been imposed on the former and
a direct subsidy paid to the latter.  Such discrimination reduces the export incentive to already established export activities.  Thus in the initial
stages, on the one hand, foreign exchange requirements are likely to increase; and on the other, since
incentives to existing exporters are blunted, capacity
to earn foreign exchange is diminished.  The resulting
frustration from these difficulties often manifests
itself in an accentuation of nationalistic and autarkic
measures.  Development on more autarkic lines suffers
from the limitations of small national markets, narrow
scope for the international division of labor, limited
exploitation of economies of scale and the more in-
tangible disadvantages of what is sometimes called
inward-looking development like the effects on learning
and the acquisition of skills.[3]  Although being ex-
posed to the breeze of competition and to the chal-
lenges of world markets is not an unmixed blessing,
there are some benefits such as improved communication
with advanced countries, increasing returns and
economies of scale, and in particular the impact of
outward-looking policies on the quality of human resources and on the ability to draw on the available
stock of knowledge.  The drawbacks are more serious,
the smaller the protected national market.


## REGIONAL CUSTOMS UNIONS

What is needed is some arrangement that, while
fostering alternative activities, will increase the

size of the market and help to economize in (or generate more) foreign exchange.

One possibility is to increase the size of the internal market by the formation of regional customs unions, and thus exploit, in an admittedly limited area, the international division of labor and economies of scale.  This has been taken up by several of the smaller coffee-producing countries.  The coffee producers of East Africa, Uganda, Kenya and Tanzania,* belong to the East African Community; and in Central America, Guatemala and El Salvador, together with Honduras, Nicaragua and Costa Rica formed the Central American Common Market (CACM).

The East African Community has its roots in the colonial period when the three territories were jointly administered and shared a common market in which there was free movement of goods and factors of production and a common currency, as well as a common external tariff and common excise duties.  In the post-independence period there was a certain loosening of the ties as national policies conflicted with regional interdependence.[4]  For instance, the common currencies were replaced by three national currencies; and, more seriously, Tanzania introduced quantitative restrictions on intra-East African trade in 1964 and 1965.  Nevertheless, intra-East African trade continued to be very important.  The figures in Table 17 may be contrasted with the 4 per cent of their exports, which on average the countries of Africa sell to other African countries.[5]

In the period 1960-65 exports between the three East African countries grew about three times the rate of exports between less-developed countries as a whole, at 12 per cent per annum compared with about 4 per cent per annum.  This was also more than twice as fast as the rate of growth of East African exports to the rest of the world.

-------------------

*Strictly speaking one should refer to Tanganyika, since Zanzibar is not a member.

TABLE 17

East African Exports 1959-66
(£ million)

| | Intra-East African[a] | To Rest of World[b] | Intra-East African Total Exports (%) |
|---|---|---|---|
| 1959 | 20.1 | 128.8 | 13.5 |
| 1960 | 22.8 | 139.7 | 14.0 |
| 1961 | 25.0 | 133.6 | 15.8 |
| 1962 | 26.8 | 139.6 | 16.1 |
| 1963 | 31.4 | 170.7 | 15.5 |
| 1964 | 40.8 | 191.3 | 18.4 |
| 1965 | 45.0 | 180.1 | 20.0 |
| 1966 | 43.9 | 214.0 | 17.0 |

[a]Excluding Zanzibar.
[b]Including re-exports.

Source: A. Hazlewood, "The Treaty for East African Cooperation" Standard Bank Review (September 1967), Table 1, pp. 3-12.

Interregional trade within CACM has increased even more rapidly. The CACM is a much more recent creation: Its roots can be traced back to the fifties but it was not until 1963 that all five members had joined. Since then interregional trade has responded with amazing dynamism (see Table 18). Exports within CACM grew on average at 24 per cent per annum in the five years after (and including) 1963, whereas in the decade 1951-61 the average growth rate of intraregional trade had been about 14 per cent. About two thirds of this trade is in manufactured, mainly consumer, goods.[6]

Although they may be successful in increasing intraregional trade, such schemes for regional integration between less-developed countries are difficult to sustain. The main reason is the fear of the least-developed members that they are being deprived of development opportunities, coupled with the fear of the more-advanced members that they will have to contribute to assisting the more backward. In both the East African Community and the CACM uneven distribution of the economic gains has created serious problems. In the case of East Africa the benefits were concentrated in Kenya, particularly around Nairobi.[7] Kenya came to account for 60 per cent of total regional trade and for 60 per cent of all manufacturing industry serving the regional market. In intra-East African trade in manufactures, as in intra-East African trade as a whole, Kenya had a large surplus and Tanzania and Uganda large deficits. Attempts at "equalization" through a system of fiscal redistribution from Kenya to the other two members were made in the early sixties but proved unsatisfactory to Tanzania and Uganda.[8] Subsequently the principle of free trade within the community was breached by the Treaty for East African Cooperation (1967), which made provision for a system of "transfer taxes" enabling the industrially less-developed members to impose what is in effect a tariff on imports of manufactures from the relatively more-developed members in order to protect their own manufacturing industry.

Within the CACM there was considerable industrialization in Guatemala and El Salvador, the two

TABLE 18

CACM Exports and Imports, 1963-67
(Values in millions of U.S. dollars)

| | EXPORTS | | | IMPORTS | | |
|---|---|---|---|---|---|---|
| | Intra-CACM | Total | Intra-CACM / Total | Intra-CACM | Total | Intra-CACM / Total |
| 1963 | 69 | 586 | 11.8% | 67 | 652 | 10.3% |
| 1964 | 105 | 672 | 15.6% | 107 | 770 | 13.9% |
| 1965 | 133 | 759 | 17.5% | 136 | 890 | 15.3% |
| 1966 | 170 | 837 | 20.3% | 176 | 936 | 18.8% |
| 1967 | 205 | 850 | 24.1% | 213 | 1,031 | 20.7% |

Source: International Monetary Fund and International Bank of Reconstruction and Development, Direction of Trade Annual 1963-67.

most advanced members, while the two least developed,
Honduras and Nicaragua, became markets for expensive
manufactures from the others without being able to
increase by much the intraregional exports of their
traditional agricultural commodities (for liberalization of agricultural trade proved an intractable
problem). Perhaps the greatest beneficiaries were
the foreign-owned manufacturing enterprises that were
set up in large numbers behind the sheltering tariff
wall.[9] Most of these were "final touch" industries,
in some cases doing little more than bottling or
packing. By 1969 the unequal distribution of the
benefits had become the key issue and for a time
Nicaragua introduced levies on regional imports in
contravention to the CACM Treaty. 1971 sees the CACM
on the edge of breakdown following the hostilities
(albeit short-lived) between Honduras and El Salvador.
Honduras has witdrawn from CACM and the four remaining
members have failed to agree on the next steps.[10]


## EXCHANGE RATE ARRANGEMENTS

Another possibility is to try to make the new
products competitive in world markets by appropriate
exchange rate arrangements. But the traditionally
advocated remedy--a depreciation of the exchange
rate--does not solve the problem. The traditional
exports of primary products will tend to be in
inelastic supply in the short run (and demand will
be inelastic in the long run for large countries)
and depreciation, unaccompanied by an increase in
export taxes, will inflate prices and incomes in
this sector. This may be justified if expansion of
production or re-equipment and modernization are
wanted. But world demand is normally not such as
to warrant expansion of primary products, except by
small countries that encroach upon the market shares
of large ones. In the case of coffee, the scope
for encroachment is in any case limited by the
International Agreement. The inflation of the incomes
of the coffee exporters and other exporters of primary
goods (such as cotton or sisal) following devaluation
will raise their demand for food and may, in some
cases, reduce its supply (e.g., by the transfer of
land from food to coffee or cotton production). In

In addition to this, the higher domestic costs of imported industrial outputs and the resulting wage-cost inflation will soon tend to wipe out the cost advantages gained by devaluation. Conventional anti-inflationary policies of restriction of domestic demand cannot tackle this type of inflation. If pursued vigorously enough, they create unemployment without touching the imported inflation in the traditional export sector and lead to the coexistence of unemployment and inflation.

The appropriate solution is to apply different remedies to staple exports, the prices of which are largely determined by world demand, and to manufactured exports, whose prices are determined by costs of production. One method is the adoption of a dual exchange rate: One fixed and higher (i.e., more units of foreign currency for one unit of domestic currency) for traditional primary exports and essential imports such as certain capital goods, industrial raw materials and food; the other lower (i.e., fewer units of foreign currency for one unit of domestic currency) and possibly floating or frequently adjusted, for new, especially manufactured, infant-industry exports and inessential or less-essential imports. The low rate might be left to equilibrate the forces of supply and demand and might rise as exports earnings from new activities rise with growing production and competitiveness.

By the employment of a dual exchange rate, export prices could be rendered competitive, while inflation of the income of the growers of primary products would be avoided.[11] This would also prevent the inflation from being communicated to the prices of home-produced food and to industrial wages, and thus avoid the danger of wiping out the benefits of exchange rate depreciation.

This type of proposal has considerable attractions for coffee-exporting countries. It has a clear advantage over a system of foreign exchange rationing and licensing, which imposes strains on a country's administration, and it harnesses the powerful incentive of profit and fear of loss to the objectives

of development planning.  The appropriate rate of
exchange for coffee could be chosen at a level that
equilibrates the supply of coffee to the quote allocated to the country under the International Coffee
Agreement.

It might be argued that a third rate, interme-
diate between the high and the low one, should be
applied to exports of nonrestricted primary products
(for which world demand shows a greater elasticity
than for coffee), where the quota reduces it to zero
for price reductions if nonquota markets are disre-
garded.  Indeed, a purist might argue that multiple
rates (or better still a set of indirect taxes and
subsidies) should be chosen so as to reap the maximum
benefits for the nation of different demand and supply
inelasticities.  But, quite apart from the rules of
the International Monetary Fund and possible foreign
retaliation, it would not be desirable to proliferate
the number of exchange rates because avoidance and
evasion would be made easier, particularly as the
dual rate can be supplemented by a system of indirect
taxes and subsidies.

While the high rate would be chosen for primary
export commodities, the low rate, which could be more
flexible and allowed to float, would apply to all
those imports that do not qualify for a currency
allocation at the official rate.  Importers would
obtain an import licence by purchasing the necessary
amount of foreign exchange.  The range of goods that
would be covered by this rate could be varied by the
government from time to time and the free rate could
thereby be influenced.  Manufacturers unwilling to
shoulder the risks of the variable rate would be able
to buy foreign exchange forward.  The government may
have to set up a purchasing agency or a marketing
board in order to ensure that the foreign exchange
proceeds of the primary exports are surrendered at
the official rate.  To avoid foreign exchange allo-
cations for the specified imports being used for other
purposes, the government could ask for advance deposits
in local currency.

Table 19 gives some indication of what the categories might be.  It shows the proportion of primary

exports (A.1) in total merchandise exports of six
coffee-exporting countries, and the proportion of
manufacturing and semimanufacturing exports (A.2).
It also attempts a rough division of imports according
to whatever domestic substitutes can be produced or
not (B.1 and B.2). It is suggested that the high
rate of exchange be applied to categories A.1 and B.2
and the low rate to categories A.2 and B.1.

Against the advantages of a system of dual exchange rates must be set at least three disadvantages.
If they were designed to stimulate manufacturing, the
stimulus to manufacturing industries would not be
uniform, but would favor those making plentiful use
of the imports admitted at low prices. Thus if all
primary products were allowed into the country at
the favorable rate chosen for "essentials", oil re-
fineries, for example, would benefit; cotton spinning
would be favored compared with weaving and clothing.
If capital goods were permitted at the low rate, this
would give an undersirable encouragement to imported-
capital-intensive methods of production. Exports
using much of the favored imported inputs would be
encouraged, compared with those using fewer or none.
On the other hand, to keep the price of imported
food low will favor labor-using industries and this
will be desirable.

A second possible objection is that dual exchange
rates, which permit imports of food and raw materials
at low prices, discourage the local production of
these goods, unless special measures are taken to
subsidize local producers, e.g., by a system of de-
ficiency payments. It has been argued that domestic
agricultural production should not be penalized in
this way. Although for some countries, like India
and Pakistan, food imports will be of decreasing
importance as development proceeds, the case for a
dual rate is probably weaker on the import side than
on the side of exports. The argument then reduces
to a case for subsidies to exports or manufacturing
industry or particular factors of production or
activities or services.[12]

One complication of export subsidies must be
noted. It may become profitable to import the item

**TABLE 19**

TRADE STRUCTURE OF SIX COFFEE-EXPORTING COUNTRIES, 1964-65
(Values in millions of U.S. dollars)

| Category | SITC No. | KENYA Products | KENYA Value | KENYA % of Total | TANZANIA[a] Products | TANZANIA[a] Value | TANZANIA[a] % of Total | COLOMBIA Products | COLOMBIA Value | COLOMBIA % of Total | EL SALVADOR Products | EL SALVADOR Value | EL SALVADOR % of Total | GUATEMALA[b] Products | GUATEMALA[b] Value | GUATEMALA[b] % of Total | COSTA RICA Products | COSTA RICA Value | COSTA RICA % of Total |
|---|---|---|---|---|---|---|---|---|---|---|---|---|---|---|---|---|---|---|---|
| A Total Merchandise Exports | | | 131.6 | 100 | | 182.8 | 100 | | 543.6 | 100 | | 183.4 | 100 | | 186.3 | 100 | | 112.8 | 100 |
| A.1 Total Agricultural Exports | | | 107.5 | 82 | | 160.2 | 82 | | 421.4 | 78 | | 150.6 | 82 | | 160.2 | 86 | | 96.3 | 85 |
| First Product | | Coffee | 41.3 | 31 | Sisal | 50.6 | 28 | Coffee | 369.2 | 68 | Coffee | 94.2 | 51 | Coffee | 92.2 | 50 | Coffee | 47.3 | 42 |
| Second Product | | Tea | 17.0 | 13 | Cotton | 30.9 | 17 | Bananas | 15.5 | 3 | Cotton | 37.5 | 20 | Cotton | 33.9 | 18 | Bananas | 28.4 | 25 |
| Third Product | | Sisal | 13.8 | 10 | Coffee | 27.5 | 15 | Tobacco | 8.3 | 2 | Sugar | 3.2 | 2 | Sugar | 6.5 | 3 | Sugar | 5.3 | 5 |
| Other Agricultural | | | 35.4 | 27 | | 51.2 | 28 | | 28.4 | 5 | | 15.7 | 9 | | 27.6 | 15 | | 15.3 | 13 |
| A.2 Total Nonagricultural Exports | | | 24.1 | 18 | | 22.6 | 12 | | 122.2 | 22 | | 32.8 | 18 | | 26.1 | 14 | | 16.5 | 15 |
| First Products | | Fuels | 9.8 | 7 | Diamonds | 19.4 | 10 | Petroleum | 81.6 | 15 | Textiles | 8.4 | 5 | Textiles | 5.4 | 3 | Fertilizer | 5.2 | 5 |
| Second Product | | Cement | 2.4 | 2 | Tanning | 1.3 | 1 | Textiles | 9.5 | 2 | Chemicals | 6.6 | 4 | Essential oils and perfumes | 4.8 | 3 | Clothing | 1.6 | 1 |
| Third Product | | Sodium carbonate | 2.1 | 2 | Cordage | 0.4 | - | Leather goods | 3.4 | - | Clothing & footwear | 4.0 | 2 | Clothing & footwear | 3.8 | 2 | Plywood | 1.1 | 1 |
| Other Nonagricultural | | | 9.8 | 7 | | 1.5 | 1 | | 27.7 | 5 | | 13.8 | 7 | | 12.1 | 6 | | 8.6 | 8 |
| B Total Merchandise Imports | | | 231.6 | 100 | | 131.4 | 100 | | 519.8 | 100 | | 195.8 | 100 | | 229.0 | 100 | | 158.4 | 100 |
| B.1 Import Substitutes[c] | | | 72.7 | 31 | | 58.8 | 45 | | 49.6 | 10 | | 42.6 | 22 | | 45.8 | 20 | | 29.8 | 20 |
| Food, Drink, Tobacco and Animal and Vegetable Oils | 0,1,4 | | 27.8 | 12 | | 9.8 | 8 | | 43.1 | 8 | | 29.4 | 15 | | 24.8 | 11 | | 15.3 | 10 |
| Textiles | 65 | | 44.9 | 19 | | 49.0 | 37 | | 6.5 | 1 | | 13.2 | 1 | | 21.0 | 9 | | 14.5 | 9 |
| B.2 Nonreproducible Imports[c] | | | 131.6 | 57 | | 71.3 | 54 | | 385.5 | 74 | | 112.0 | 57 | | 139.9 | 61 | | 93.9 | 59 |
| Fuels | 3 | | 27.4 | 12 | | 4.9 | 4 | | 8.5 | 2 | | 11.4 | 6 | | 15.9 | 7 | | 8.4 | 5 |
| Chemicals | 5 | | 21.2 | 9 | | 9.9 | 7 | | 84.3 | 16 | | 35.1 | 18 | | 38.5 | 17 | | 25.8 | 16 |
| Capital Goods | 67,68,69, 7, ex8 | | 83.0 | 36 | | 56.5 | 43 | | 292.7 | 56 | | 65.5 | 33 | | 85.8 | 37 | | 59.7 | 38 |
| Iron and Steel | 67 | | 12.5 | 5 | | 7.9 | 6 | | 38.3 | 7 | | 6.9 | 3 | | 10.7 | 4 | | 8.0 | 5 |
| Machinery | ex71,72 | | 32.1 | 14 | | 23.0 | 18 | | 165.9 | 32 | | 35.4 | 18 | | 43.0 | 19 | | 32.9 | 21 |
| Transport Equipment[d] | ex73 | | 16.6 | 7 | | 13.4 | 10 | | 56.8 | 11 | | 11.0 | 6 | | 15.3 | 7 | | 7.4 | 5 |
| Other Nonreproducible Imports | 68,69, ex8 | | 21.8 | 10 | | 12.2 | 9 | | 32.7 | 6 | | 12.2 | 6 | | 16.5 | 7 | | 11.4 | 7 |
| BC Other Imports | ex2,60-64,66, ex8,9 | | 27.3 | 12 | | 1.3 | 1 | | 84.7 | 16 | | 41.2 | 21 | | 43.3 | 19 | | 34.7 | 22 |

[a] Tanganyika only.
[b] 1965 only.
[c] The categories are to some extent arbitrary and should be considered indicative only.
[d] Excluding automobiles.

Source: U.N., _International Trade Statistics_ (1965).

at international prices and to re-export it, claiming
the subsidy.  This depends on whether the subsidy is
large enough to outweigh transport and handling costs
(goods are imported c.i.f. but exported f.o.b.).
The same consideration applies to imported inputs.
Evidence suggests that incentives have been set up
in several less-developed countries to export items
for which the cost of inputs (evaluated at c.i.f.
cost) would exceed the value (f.o.b.) of the exports,
in international prices.[13]  Clearly export subsidies
can be too large; but as long as they are kept within
a critical limit a strong case can be made for them.

A third difficulty, on a different plane of
reasoning, which explains the reluctance to move away
from import controls that are recognized to be inef-
ficient, is the existence of tied aid.  This forms
a significant proportion of available foreign exchange
in some less-developed countries.  There are ways of
matching supplies of inconvertible currencies and
demand in a system of dual exchange rates.[14]  In any
case, aid-tying should not be accepted as an unalter-
able fact.

The increased competitiveness of manufactured
exports derived from a lowering of prices to foreign
buyers achieved in this manner has a number of additional advantages.  If the low rate is allowed to
float and thus to equilibrate the demand for and the
supply of nonessential imports with the demand for
and the supply of manufactured exports, the discount
of the floating rate (i.e., the premium on buying
foreign exchange over the official rate) will reflect
the balance between the demand for inessential imports
and the supply and the competitiveness of manufactured
exports.  The lower the rate, the greater the encouragement to exports.  If the response is an increase in
the supply of exports, this will tend to reduce the
discount and bring the two rates nearer together.

Such a system would also meet a number of difficulties that arise from the different levels of
development at which different developing countries
find themselves.  Differences among less-developed
countries, which have  tended to increase in the last

few years, can present problems similar in nature to
those between less-developed and developed countries.
A system of simple preferences for manufactured imports, without a number of safeguards for the least
developed, may simply award the lion's share of the
markets to those less-developed countries already
more advanced and therefore least in need of assistance.

A system of dual rates, with one rate floating
to equilibrate the demand for foreign exchange for
less essential imports with the supply of foreign
exchange earned by manufacturing exports, would automatically adjust the handicap to the level of industrialization.  The least-developed countries at the
earliest stage of industrialization would enjoy the
greatest price advantages for manufactured exports,
while those whose cost conditions approximate those
of the industrial countries would find their discount
dwindling away.

In addition, it would encourage trade between
developing countries without, once again, jeopardizing
the chances of the least-developed countries of parti-
cipating in industrialization.  As we have seen, it
is a common failing of schemes of regional integration
among developing countries that some member countries
not only fail to share in the benefits of industrialization, but are deprived of the opportunities that
protection would have given them.  The proposed system
would combine the benefits of regional integration
with those of participation in the industrialization
process of the least developed and would thus remove
what has been a main drawback in plans of integration
between countries.

A system of indirect taxes and subsidies can be
used to achieve the same effects as a dual exchange
rate, although it may be more difficult to administer.
Traditional exports and inessential imports are taxed
and the tax revenue is used to subsidize manufacturing
exports and essential imports.  One component in such
a strategy is already provided by the export taxes
and levies on coffee, which the majority of producing
countries employ in one form or another.[15]  If coffee

were the only or the main export crop, a single,
across-the-broad devaluation or depreciation, combined
with an increase in the export tax on coffee, would
achieve the same result as a dual rate.  While manufacturing activity for export is stimulated, the rise
in the price of coffee expressed in domestic currency
is creamed off as tax revenue.  The revenue can be
used to subsidize essential imports whose domestic
prices have risen and in particular farm implements
and fertilizers for the production of food, and to
give additional incentives to manufacturing exports.

Finally, the same objective can be achieved by
a national central marketing agency that buys coffee
and possibly other primary products at low prices
and sells them at higher prices in world markets.
The agency would have to have the right of monopoly
purchase from the farmers.  The agency may also provide other services to the farmers.  The case for
such marketing agencies is stronger, the more important it is to fix different prices for different
primary exports, and the weaker the case for admitting
imports at a high rate.

It is easier to recommend outward-looking policies
than to implement them.  Obstacles lie both on the
side of advanced countries and on the side of developing countries and they are both economic and
noneconomic.  To raise the competitiveness of exports
is only one side of the story.  The other is the need
of importing countries to remove obstacles to trade
and to give free access to the imports of developing
countries.  It is futile, if not hypocritical, to
preach diversification while blocking markets for any
successful push into exports.  Reduced protection,
high levels of demand and high rates of growth in the
advanced countries are necessary in order to create
the demand for the exports into which the developing
countries are attempting to diversify their coffee
earnings.  It is greater outward diversification in
the trading patterns of the advanced countries that
is a necessary condition of successful diversification
in coffee-exporting countries.  If the advanced
countries were to accept the structural adjustments
imposed by better access for developing countries,

exports as readily as they already accept those imposed by technical progress--and both have precisely the same beneficial effects upon their own levels of living--one side of the problem of diversification would be solved.

Beyond trade, there are other things the developed countries can do to encourage an outward-looking, international attitude of developing countries. A more generous flow of aid, with fewer strings, on soft terms and of the right kind, would reduce pressures to close the frontiers and look inward. So would well-designed technical assistance, genuine international cooperation, a better understanding of the problems of the developing countries, greater tolerance of some of the measures that look nationalistic, like the desire for greater local participation in foreign private enterprise and a recognition of the multiplicity of roads to development without doctrinaire attachment to a particular pattern.

## NOTES

1. This is now well understood. See, e.g., C.F. Diaz-Alejandro, "On the Import Intensity of Import Substitution," Kyklos, Vol. 18 (1965), pp. 495-511.

2. International Monetary Fund, Annual Report (1966), p. 14.

3. Donald B. Keesing, "Outward-looking Policies and Economic Development," Economic Journal, Vol. LXXVII, No. 77(June, 1967) pp. 303-20.

4. See A. Segal, "The Integration of Developing Countries: Some Thoughts on East Africa and Central America," Journal of Common Market Studies, Vol. V, No.3 (March 1967), pp. 252-82.

5. See A. Hazlewood, "The Treaty for East African Cooperation," Standard Bank Review (September 1967), pp. 3-12.

6.  See Yu-Min Chou, "Economic Integration in Less Developed Countries:  The Case of Small Countries," Journal of Development Studies, Vol. III, No. 4 (July 1967), pp. 352-73.

7.  A. Segal, op. cit.

8.  A. Hazlewood, op. cit.

9.  M.S. Wionczek, "The Rise and Decline of Latin American Economic Integration," Journal of Common Market Studies, Vol. IX, No. 1  (September 1970), pp. 49-66.

10.  Latin America Newsletter (London), Vol. V, No. 7 (February 12, 1971), p. 50.

11.  See N. Kaldor, Essays on Economic Policy, Vol. II, Chapter 19(London:  Duckworth & Co., 1964), and "Dual Exchange Rates and Economic Development," Economic Bulletin for Latin America (September 1964).

12.  See Paul Streeten, "The Case for Export Subsidies," Journal for Development Studies, Vol. V, (July 1969), pp. 270-73.

13.  See Jagdish Bhagwati, The Theory and Practice of Commercial Policy:  Departures from Unified Exchange Rates, International Finance Section, Princeton University, Special Papers in International Economics, No. 8 (January 1969), p. 54.

14.  "The Implications of Economic Controls and of Liberalization," in Economic Survey of Asia and the Far East 1968 (Bangkok:  United Nations, 1969), p. 92.

15.  See FAO, The World Coffee Economy, C.B.S. 33, (1961), pp. 3-4.

PAUL STREETEN is Warden of Queen Elizabeth House, Director of the Institute of Commonwealth Studies, and Fellow of Balliol College, Oxford. He was Professor of Economics at the University of Sussex, Fellow of the Institute of Development Studies (1964-66), and Deputy Director-General of Economic Planning at the Ministry of Overseas Development (1966-68).

Mr. Streeten was a Rockefeller Fellow in the USA, Research Fellow at the Johns Hopkins University, Baltimore, and Fellow at the Center for Advanced Studies, Wesleyan University, Connecticut. He is a member of the UK National Commission of UNESCO, of the Governing Body of the Institute of Development Studies and of the Board of the Commonwealth Development Corporation. He has lectured in Japan, Trinidad, Argentina, Chile, Brazil, India, Pakistan, the Philippines, Ceylon, in several African countries and in most countries on the Continent of Europe. He has worked for international organizations and many developing countries.

Mr. Streeten holds an M.A. from the University of Aberdeen and from the University of Oxford, where he was a Scholar of Balliol College.

DIANE ELSON is a Teaching Fellow in Economics at the University of York. She was Research Assistant at the Institute of Commonwealth Studies, Oxford (1970-71).

Miss Elson holds a B.A. in Philosophy, Politics and Economics from the University of Oxford.

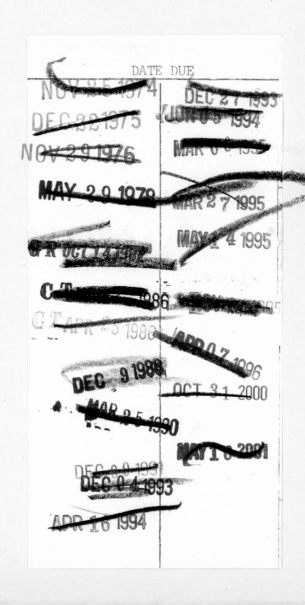